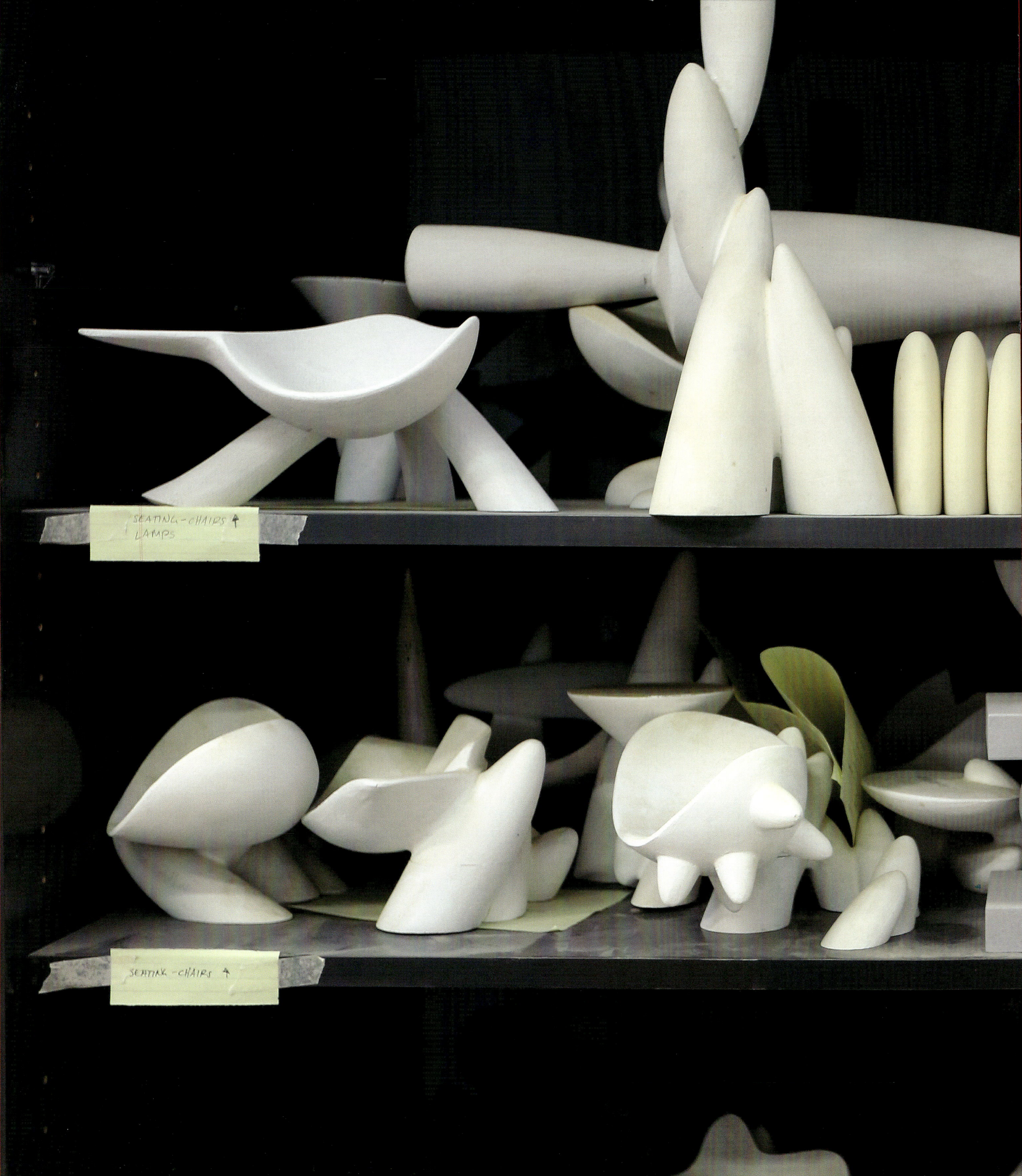
SEATING - CHAIRS &
LAMPS
SEATING - CHAIRS &

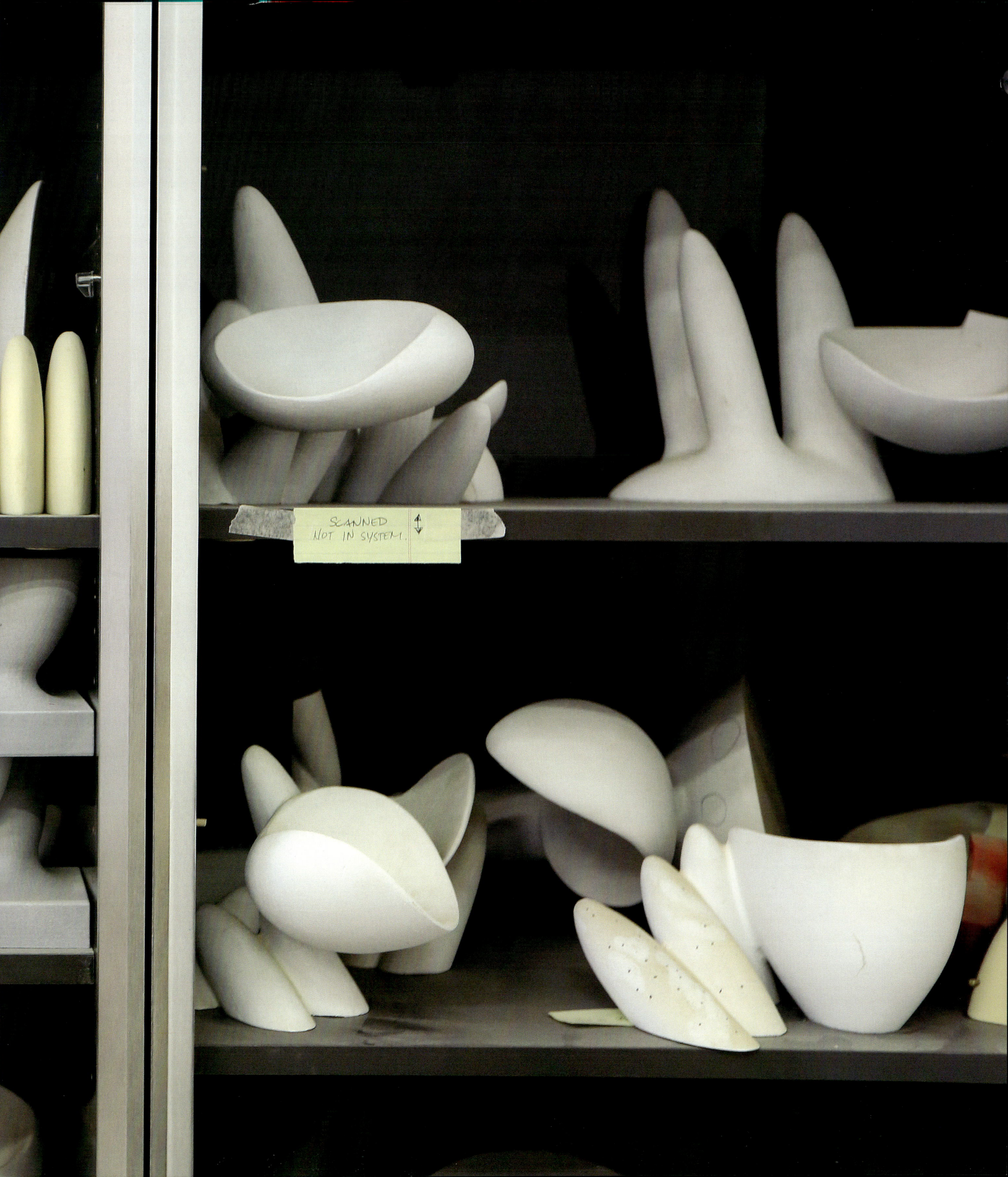
SCANNED
NOT IN SYSTEM.

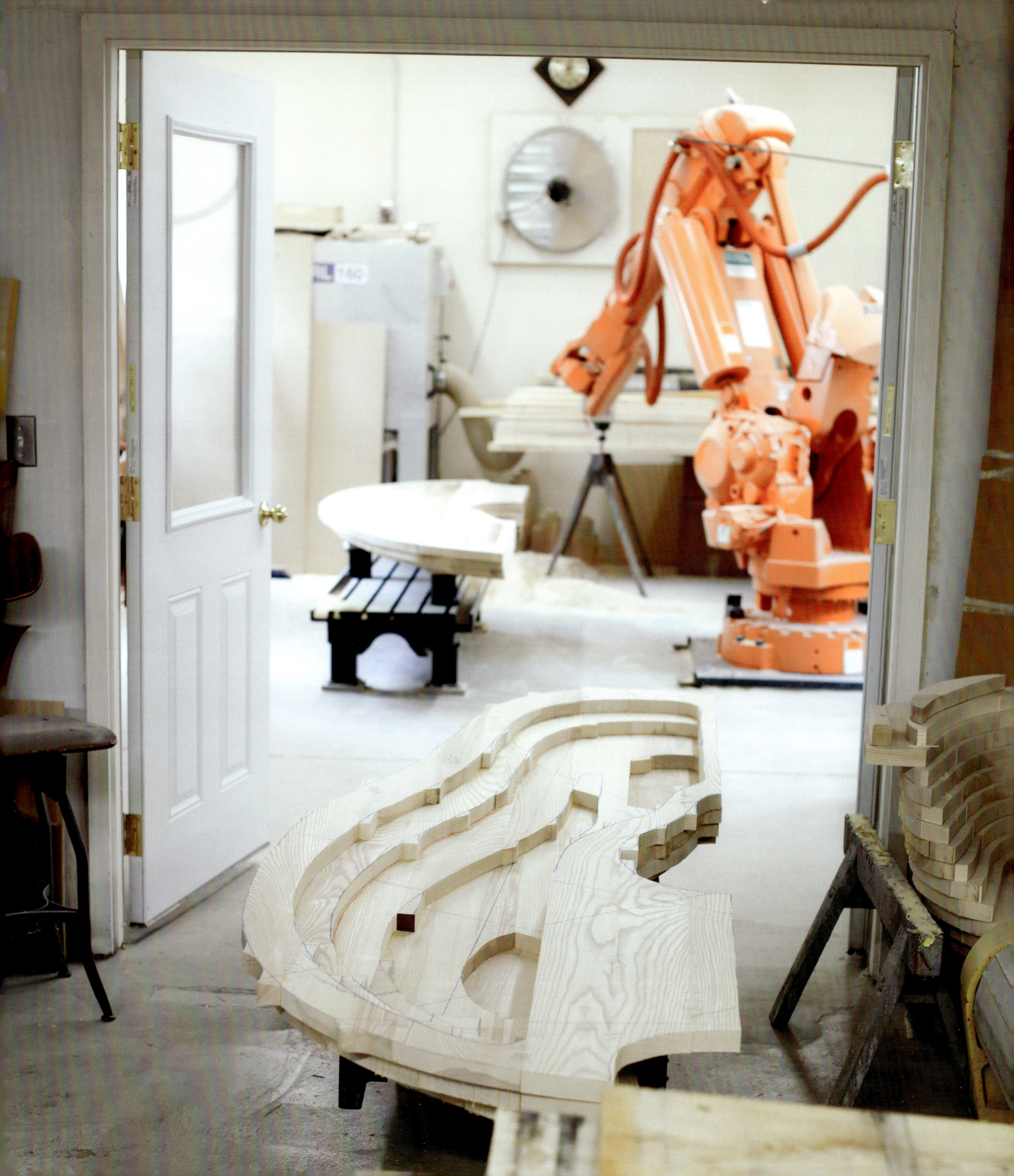

Wendell Castle Remastered

Glenn Adamson

Ronald T. Labaco

Lowery Stokes Sims

Samantha De Tillio

Amy Cheatle

Steven J. Jackson

MUSEUM OF ARTS AND DESIGN

THE ARTIST BOOK FOUNDATION

NEW YORK   LONDON

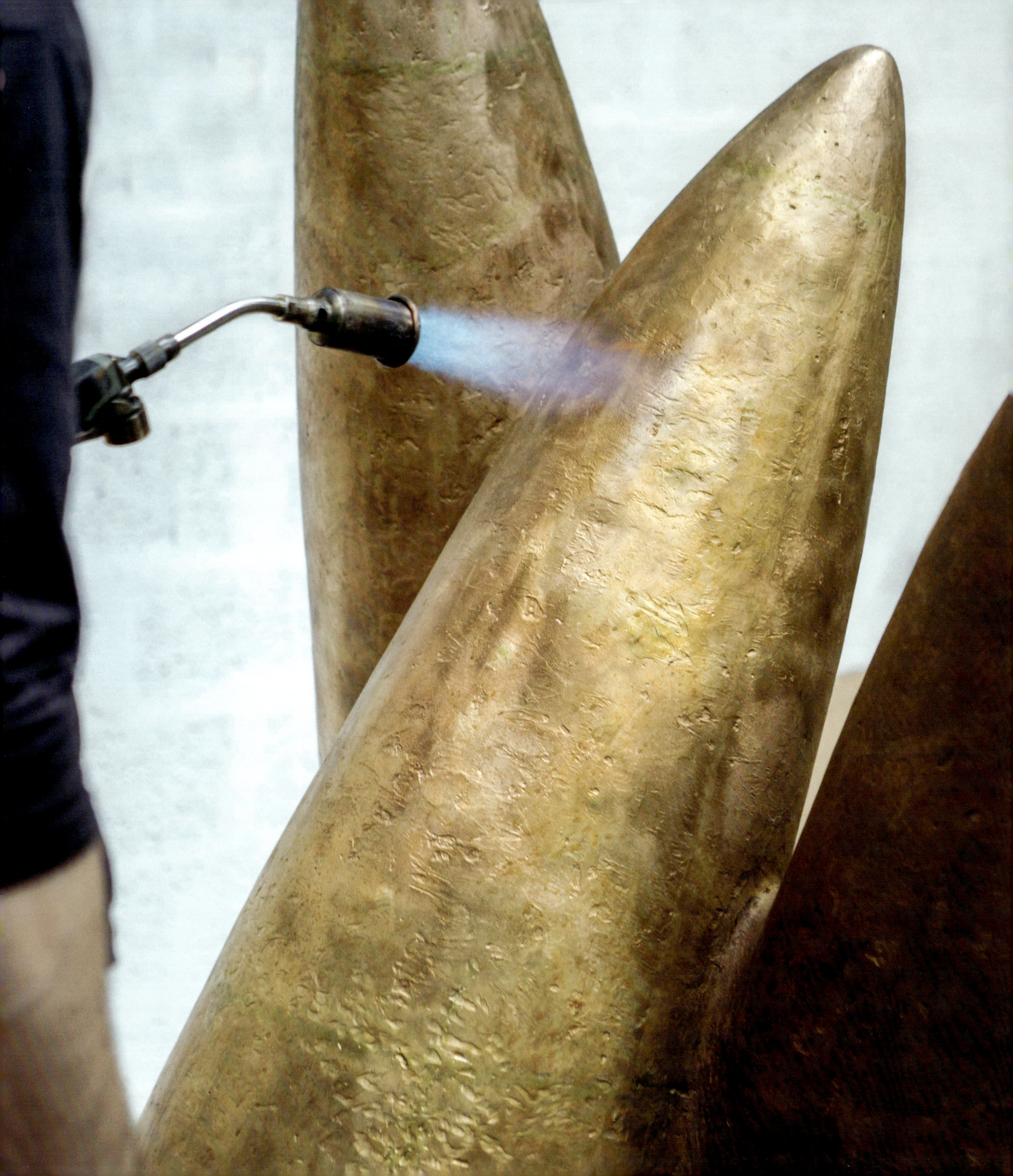

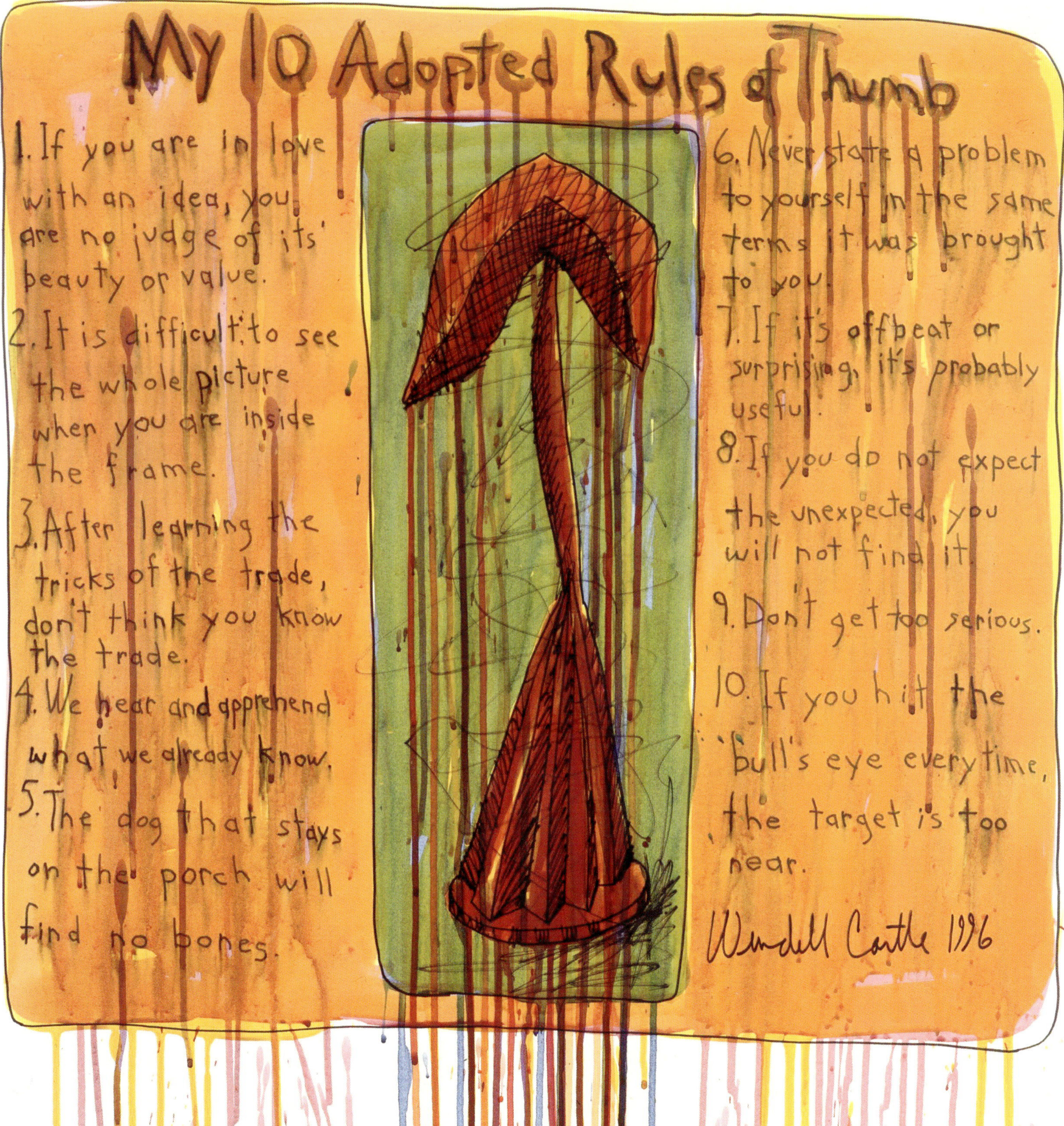

My 10 Adopted Rules of Thumb
1. If you are in love with an idea, you are no judge of its' beauty or value.
2. It is difficult to see the whole picture when you are inside the frame.
3. After learning the tricks of the trade, don't think you know the trade.
4. We hear and apprehend what we already know.
5. The dog that stays on the porch will find no bones.
6. Never state a problem to yourself in the same terms it was brought to you.
7. If it's offbeat or surprising, it's probably useful.
8. If you do not expect the unexpected, you will not find it.
9. Don't get too serious.
10. If you hit the "bull's eye every time, the target is too near.
Wendell Castle 1996

Foreword

GLENN ADAMSON

HANGING ON THE WALL OF Wendell Castle's studio in Scottsville, New York, is a poster bearing the title *My 10 Adopted Rules of Thumb*. It is a revealing list, as close to a manifesto as the artist has ever produced. Given that he is a man who typically lets his work do the talking for him, Castle's credo provides unusual and useful insight into his core values.

Several of the rules are very matter-of-fact, sitting comfortably within a long tradition of American homespun wisdom. Perhaps that is to be expected given that Castle grew up in pre–World War II Kansas, where one might have expected to hear endearingly rustic sayings such as "after learning the tricks of the trade, don't think you know the trade," or "the dog that stays on the porch will find no bones."

Elsewhere in the list Castle strikes a different note, more redolent of the East Coast *avant garde*. Rule 6, for example, is worthy of any progressive art theorist: "Never state a problem to yourself in the same terms it was brought to you." Then there is Rule 10, Castle's best-known saying and one that he has repeated in many public lectures over the years: "If you hit the bull's-eye every time, the target is too near." Here, Castle professes a vigorous experimentalism that cuts against his unpretentious practicality, a productive opposition that is indeed visible in every one of his projects.

For the purposes of this book and the project that it documents, perhaps the most important rule is the one he put right up front at Number 1: "If you are in love with an idea, you are no judge of its beauty or value." Notice how this astute, if austere, observation cuts against any singular vantage point—either of pragmatism or experimentalism. Castle seems to suggest that there is no permanently safe ground for an artist: neither the satisfying certainties of artisanal know-how, nor the thrill ride of wild conception. Once an artist has put an idea out in the world, it must be critically and objectively, maybe even suspiciously, judged—and perhaps abandoned.

A man of his word, Castle has indeed followed that demanding precept across his long career, with unpredictable forays into one idiom after another: Scandinavian modern, plasticized Pop, hyperrealistic *trompe l'oeil*, Post-Modern Neoclassicism, black-and-white Expressionism, and comic-book anthropomorphism. In the millennia-long history of furniture design, there is no one to match him in versatility. Over six decades, Castle has mounted a one-man survey of the possible.

Yet there is one moment in his career that stands paramount—or has, until recently. This was a stretch of years beginning in the early 1960s when he adopted the process of "stack lamination" to create his furniture. The technique is easily understood—in fact, it was inspired by a how-to book about carving duck decoys that he had seen when he was younger. Multiple wooden boards, each shaped as a cross section of the anticipated form, are stacked up and then glued together into a solid, stepped mass that roughly approximates the eventual desired result. The material is then carved down using a chainsaw, angle grinders, and hand tools, rendering the surface continuous. This process liberated Castle from established modes of furniture making while opening up infinite formal

Fig. 1. *My 10 Adopted Rules of Thumb*, 1996.
Acrylic and ink on paper, 111 x 129 in. (281.9 x 327.7 cm).
Courtesy of the artist.

possibilities. He could now make furniture stretch and crouch, spring and sprawl, unlimited by the dimensions of single boards or the logic of traditional construction. He was suddenly making furniture using the subtractive carving techniques of sculpture, rather than the additive techniques of joinery, and indeed his work immediately began to grapple not with the history of decorative art, but rather with the likes of Constantin Brâncuşi and Henry Moore.

Having discovered this technique, Castle might have been expected to stick with it. But he didn't. In keeping with Rule 1, he refused to "fall in love" with the idea of stack lamination or the freedoms it offered. By the late 1960s, he was already moving on, blending other methods of building into his sculptural forms, and also adopting molded plastic when few other furniture makers were using that material. (Castle has long been an early adopter.) He never entirely dropped stack lamination from his copious bag of tricks, but neither was it front and center in his practice.

But a good idea is hard to keep down. In recent years, Castle has returned to his groundbreaking ideas of the 1960s, reinventing them for the twenty-first century. Crucial to this latest phase of his career, as you will read in curator Ron Labaco's introduction, is the use of a robot to carve his work. This decision to "tool up" has been a canny move for the octogenarian artist. It has meant that, even as his physical ability to shape the wood has diminished, his sculptural powers have dramatically increased. He is still thinking with his hands, in that each new form begins with drawings and small-scale maquettes. But through technology—and the help of his studio assistants—he can now achieve dramatic scale.

With this body of work, Castle has once again reasserted his place at the forefront of innovation in furniture, even as he recalls the deep roots of his own career. *Wendell Castle Remastered* presents the new work in direct juxtaposition to his first forays into stack-laminated, sculptural furniture. We are extraordinarily proud to be able to compare these two moments of his achievement at the Museum of Arts and Design—all the more so as Castle has been such a constant presence in our galleries over the years in between. In addition to a one-person show held at our museum in 1989, he has been included in numerous other exhibitions at the institution over the years, including many of our most defining projects: the groundbreaking series of exhibitions *Young Americans,* 1962; *The American Craftsman,* 1964; *Fantasy Furniture,* 1966; *Objects: USA,* 1969; *New Handmade Furniture,* 1979; *Craft Today: Poetry of the Physical,* 1986; *Breaking Barriers: Recent American Craft,* 1995; *Objects for Use,* 2001; and *NYC Makers: The MAD Biennial,* 2014. (Although Castle is not a New York City maker, we smuggled him in by showing one of his objects in a Brooklyn-made shipping crate.)

Given this longstanding relationship, it is perhaps no surprise that *Wendell Castle Remastered* has attracted such warm and generous support from our museum's community. We are grateful to Friedman Benda, Autodesk, The Anne and Ronald Abramson Family Foundation, Ann F. Kaplan and Robert Fippinger, Susan Steinhauser and Dan Greenberg, The Margaret and Daniel Loeb – Third Point Foundation, Jane and Leonard Korman, Fleur Bresler, Anita and Ronald Wornick, Diane and Marc A. Grainer, the University of Rochester–Memorial Art Gallery, and KLM Royal Dutch Airlines for their generous support of the exhibition project. My thanks also go to Alison Castle, for having the foresight to create a documentary film on her father. MAD's ingenious and hardworking staff has nimbly maneuvered this book and the exhibition into place. I would particularly like to recognize Ron Labaco, Marcia Docter Senior Curator; Samantha De Tillio, Curatorial Assistant and Project Manager; Hendrik Gerrits, Director of Exhibitions (and designer of the show); Elizabeth Kirrane, Senior Exhibitions Manager; Willow Holdorf, Exhibitions Associate; Patrick Paine, Head Preparator; Carla Hernandez, Associate Registrar for Exhibitions; and Ellen Holdorf, Chief Registrar.

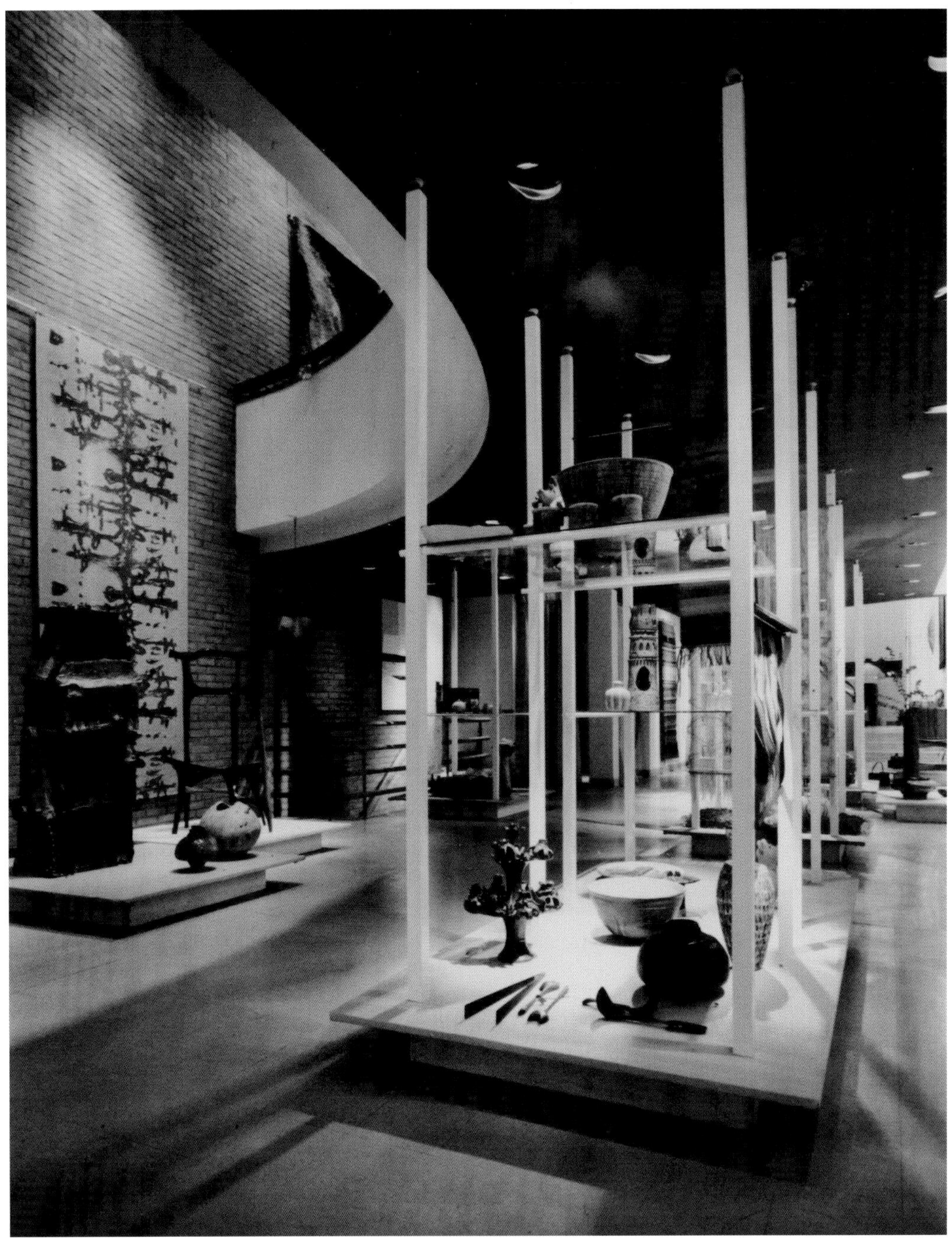

Fig. 2. Installation view of *Young Americans,* 1962, at the Museum of Contemporary Crafts showing Castle's *Scribe's Stool.* Courtesy of the American Crafts Council.

Our last and greatest thanks, of course, go to Wendell Castle himself, and his extraordinary team of artisans. They embody everything that our museum stands for: a collaborative spirit, mastery of means both analogue and digital, and an unceasing passion for discovery. Castle turned 83 this year. He has been one of America's most innovative artists since the 1950s. The truly amazing thing is— he's just getting started.

New York, NY
Winter 2015

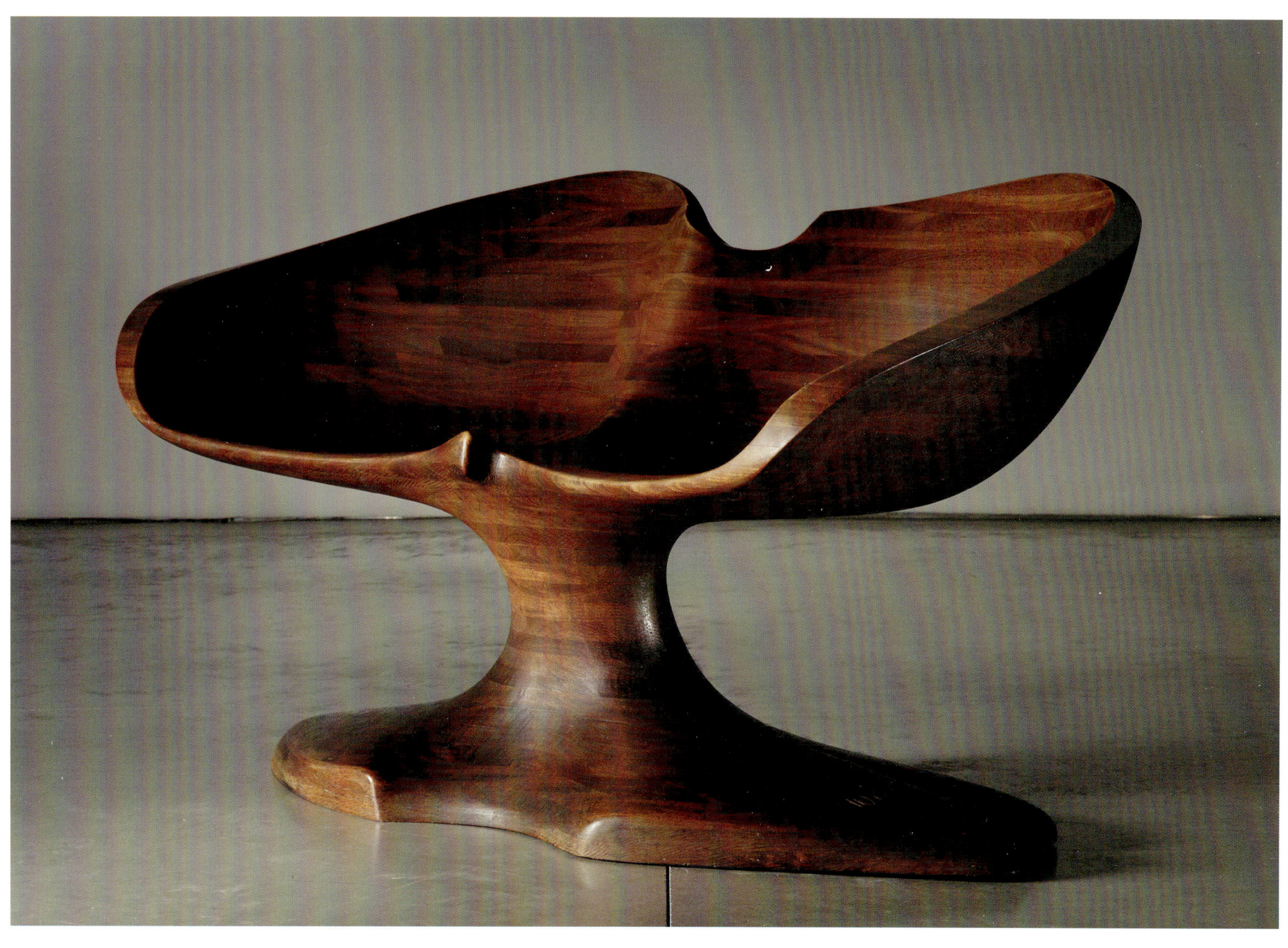

Introduction

RONALD T. LABACO

Fig. 3. *Double Chair*, 1967. Afromosia, 28 ¾ x 55 ½ x 28 in. (73 x 141 x 71.1 cm). Courtesy of Margaret and Daniel S. Loeb, New York, NY.

1. The Museum of Arts and Design was originally established in 1956 as the Museum of Contemporary Crafts. In 1987, the name was changed to the American Craft Museum and, in 2002, changed again to the Museum of Arts and Design.

2. The term "remastered" in the exhibition title *Wendell Castle Remastered* may be read as a conceit with multiple nuances. In one instance "remastered" may be read as a playful, if not entirely accurate, reference to Castle's adoption of digital tools in the creation of his new work. In media production, a remastered recording is one in which the quality of a preexisting analogue version of a video or audio recording has been enhanced using digital equipment. A second trope suggests that Castle is revisiting and strengthening his mastery of the stack-lamination technique that he originated. And a third casts Wendell Castle as a twenty-first-century "Old Master" artist in a manner similar to Medieval and Renaissance Europe, through his mastery of his medium, the presentation of a "masterwork" (*Scribe's Stool* from 1962 that received national acclaim) to the local guild, and the establishment of a workshop with journeymen and apprentice assistants who performed the more mundane tasks, such as carving, in the recognizable style of the master.

3. All quotes from Wendell Castle were drawn from a telephone interview with the artist by the author, conducted on March 5, 2014.

WENDELL CASTLE IS INTERNATIONALLY ACCLAIMED as a major figure in art furniture and design. At the age of 83, this master furniture maker, designer, sculptor, and educator is in the sixth decade of a prolific career that began in 1958, one that parallels the emergence and growth of the American studio craft movement. Castle is also inextricably linked to the Museum of Arts and Design (MAD). He has been included in twenty exhibitions over the course of the institution's history since its beginning as the Museum of Contemporary Crafts, founded by philanthropist Aileen Osborn Webb in 1956.[1] Castle's *Scribe's Stool* (1960–1961, plate 2) was featured in the museum's 1962 exhibition, *Young Americans*, and illustrated in the museum's magazine, *Craft Horizons*. Inclusion in this show led to Castle's appointment later that year as a professor with the School for American Craftsmen, also founded by Webb, at the Rochester Institute of Technology (RIT) in Rochester, New York. While there, he would establish his studio and primary residence in nearby Scottsville, where he continues to work and live today.

This mutual relationship between maker and museum comes full circle in *Wendell Castle Remastered*.[2] In this exhibition, Wendell Castle casts a critical eye toward the first decade of his own artistic production by creating a new body of work that revisits, through a contemporary lens, his achievements in the pioneering use of stack lamination in the 1960s. This self-reflective meditation examines a crucial period during which Castle's sculptural practices came to define his pivotal role as a leader in the field and set the foundation for his longevity.

Based on a selection of historically significant works chosen by the museum, Castle has produced new works through his latest practice of combining handcraftsmanship—such as carving, rasping, and finishing—with digital technologies that include 3D scanning and modeling, and computer-controlled milling. Castle's experimentation with the tools of digital fabrication in stack lamination began incrementally in 2011, but almost everything that he makes today utilizes these digital technologies. These new works are installed in dialogue with the earlier pieces that inspired them as a study of comparisons and contrasts in form, scale, volume, and visual language.

Castle's interest in revisiting his use of stack lamination—a method of fabrication that he had introduced to his furniture in 1963, but which was no longer his primary focus by 1970—began as a mental exercise in 2005. In a recent interview he explained:

About nine or ten years ago, I was kind of looking over what I was doing and where I was going and thought to myself, what would I do if I didn't have any assistants? I thought, well, that's exactly the way it was when I started. I didn't have any assistants. And I thought, what is truly me about my work? And what is unique about my work?[3]

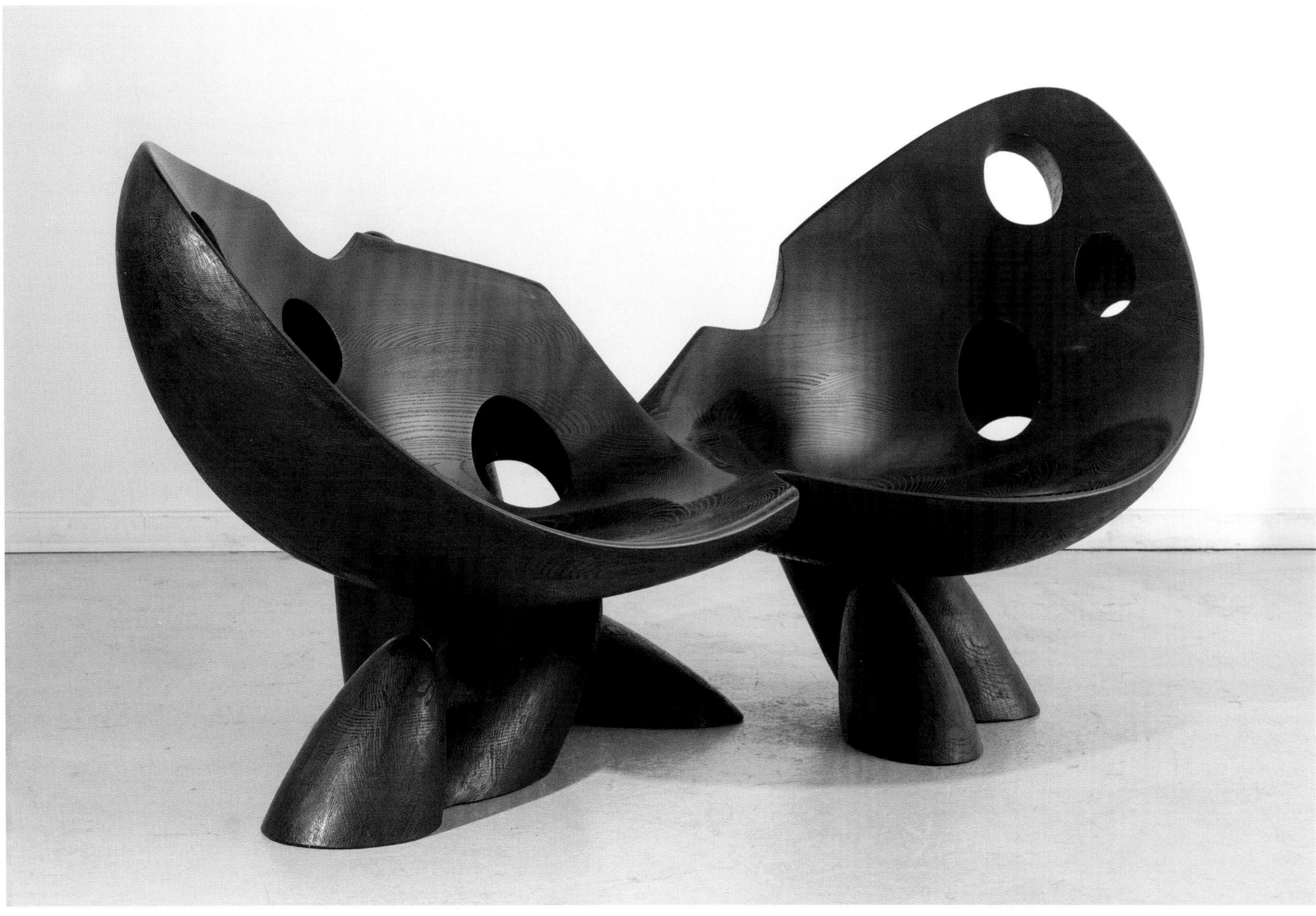

Fig. 4. *Grand Whispers*, 2013. Stained ash, 40 1/10 x 79 ¾ x 38 ¼ in. (101.9 x 202.6 x 97.2 cm). Courtesy of the artist and Friedman Benda, New York, NY.

Castle has always employed studio assistants since the establishment of his first workshop. By trying to imagine his studio without assistants, it situated him in the same circumstance as when he began his career. At the outset, Castle made each piece of furniture by himself. It was only with more experience and success that he could begin to think about employing his first studio assistant, a talented student in one of his classes who showed promise, to carry out the more mundane tasks such as gluing or carving, rasping, and other surface treatments that could be reproduced in his style by a talented artisan.

Trained as an industrial designer and a sculptor, in the beginning Castle was not familiar with the tools or techniques of traditional woodworking. Rather, he applied the implements on hand—atypical electric tools used in the production of modern wood and stone sculpture—to realize his work:

> *And I used different tools than woodworkers used. My main tools in the '60s and they are still main tools today, to some extent, are the chainsaw and ball mills and pneumatic chisels, all things that would be normally associated with sculpture, not normally associated with furniture making.*

Therefore, by extension, it seemed perfectly logical for Castle to explore new possibilities in stack lamination using the most advanced tools available today, namely the computer-assisted fabrication technologies of 3D scanning, modeling, and printing, as well as CNC milling, which he started to do in 2011.

Further reflection upon those questions in 2005 led Castle to reinvestigate the stack-lamination process that had become his signature style in the 1960s. His development of this technique and its application to furniture is arguably one of the most significant contributions to studio furniture in the late postwar era. While this method of production had been explored in fine art by wood sculptors, it was a distinct contrast from traditional furniture making and cabinetry, and had even drawn criticism from established woodworkers such as George Nakashima, Wharton Esherick, and Sam Maloof.

Even as a sculpture student I had known about lamination. But the lamination that I'd known about was quite different. Sculptors would have a millwork house glue them up, this really giant block of wood or whatever shape they needed, a rectangle for a figure, say. And I thought how I could streamline that process by being able to imagine cross sections through the piece so you could precut the wood. And you wouldn't have to do all this carving before you were anywhere near the form. And so that was my contribution to laminating. But laminating eliminated that need to know how to do woodworking. I didn't have to know how to veneer or cut dovetail joints or do any marquetry or anything, any of that stuff. I could just glue together large shapes of wood and carve them. And it turned out that that was really a breakthrough.

Fig. 5. *Crossroads*, 2014. Stained ash, each: 38 1/10 x 83 x 41 1/10 in. (96.8 x 210.8 x 104.5 cm). Courtesy of the Pizzuti Collection.

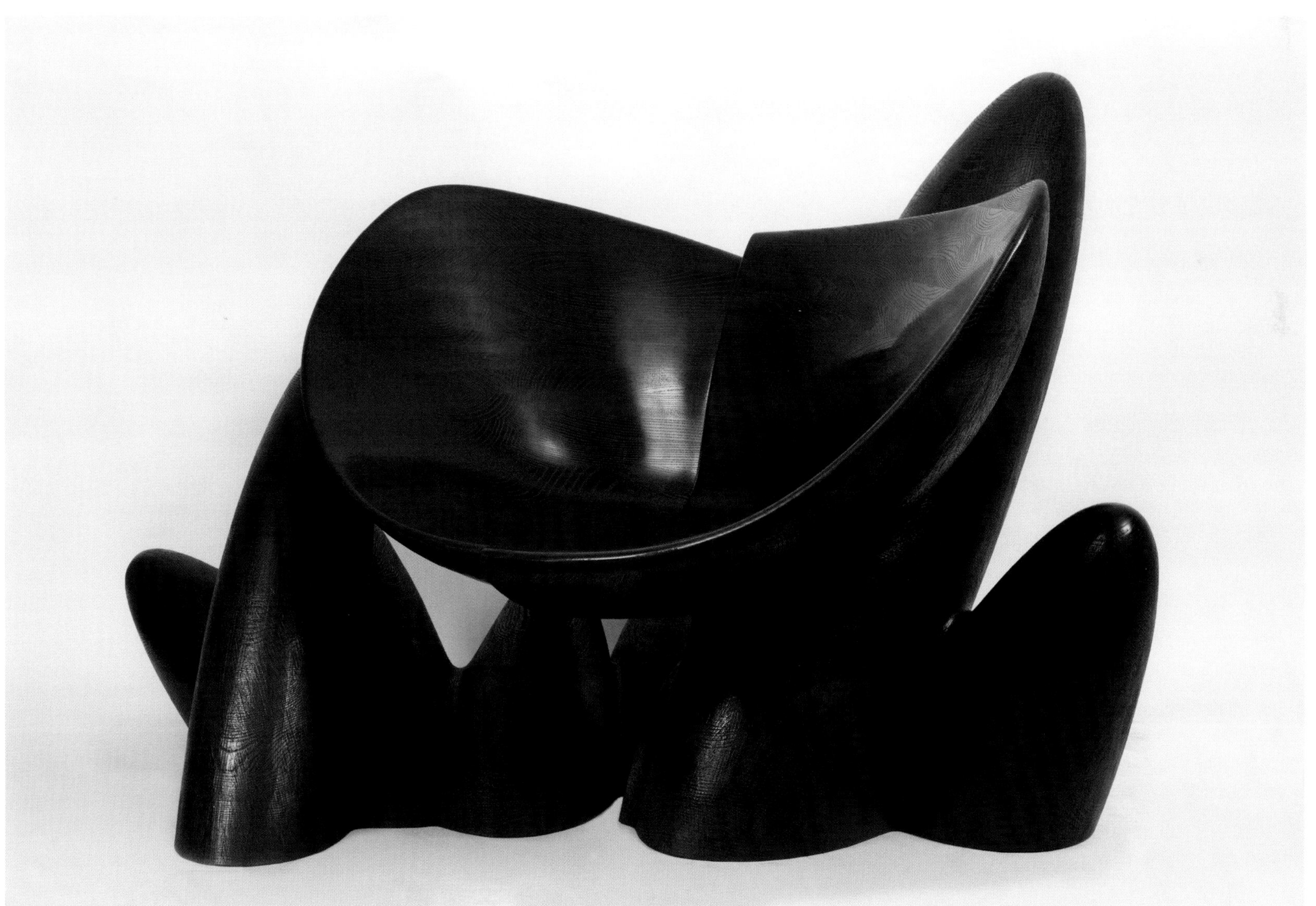

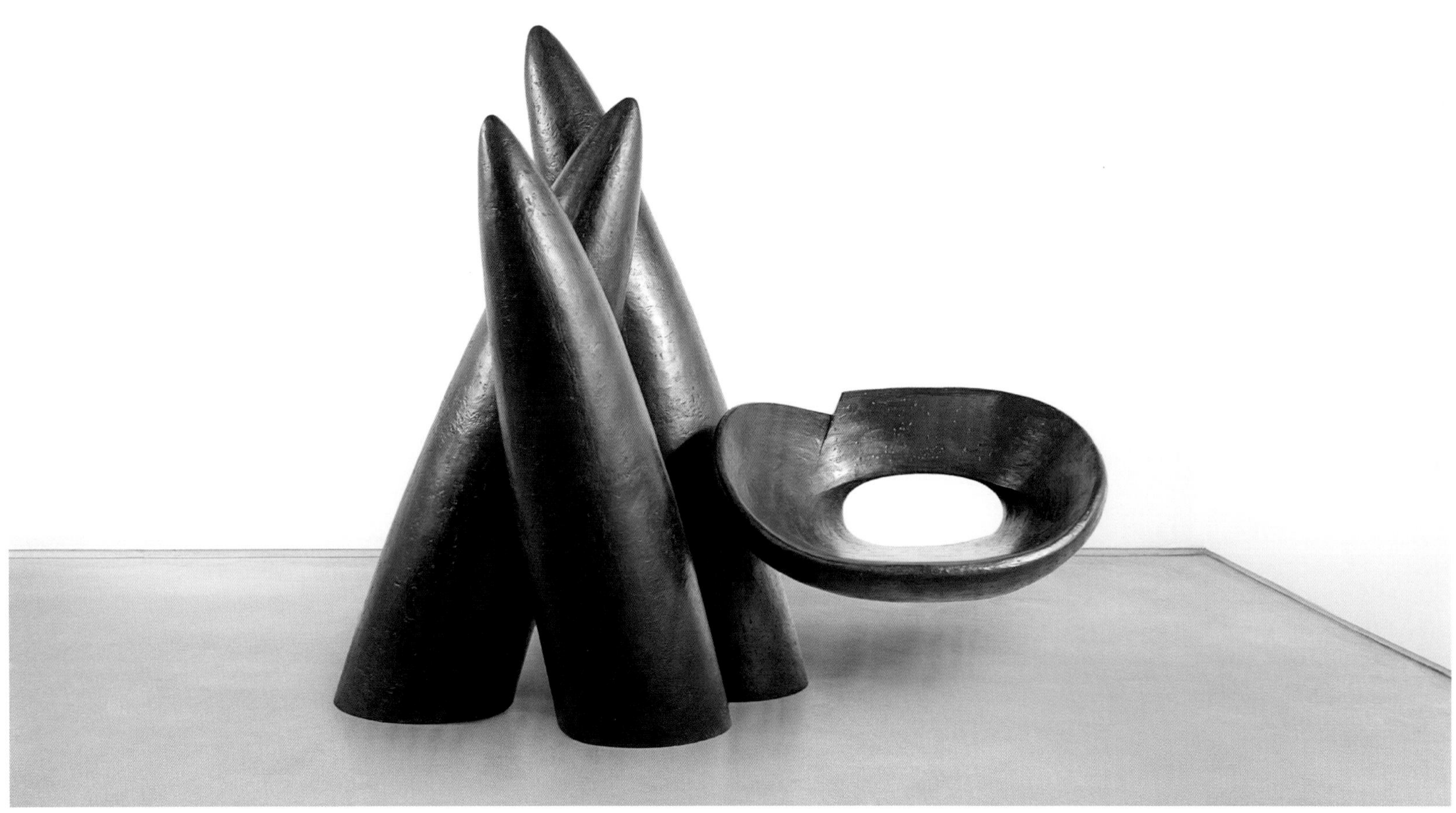

Castle's technique liberated him from the rectilinear forms of frame-and-panel construction and mortise-and-tenon joinery, and it allowed him to work in a manner akin to sculpture. The method also allowed for the creation of volumetric forms in the round, a vocabulary of softly organic shapes, and the invention of new furniture hybrids such as a chair-table, all themes that are explored in the exhibition.

But how does Castle's approach to stack lamination today differ from fifty years ago? He explained:

And so in looking back, all those things were right. And continue to be right today. I was still inter-ested in soft, organic forms. I was still interested in volume. I still wanted to make multifunctional pieces. But nowadays, with the technology available, I can approach it entirely differently and have it much more complex. Those are some of the things that have changed. Scanning and 3D modeling and robotic carving and 3D printing—those are perfect things for what I'm doing.

I used to—I mean, I still think and believe very strongly in this, that the idea parts of these things ought to be done on pencil and paper, not on the computer…. So, that part hasn't changed a bit. I draw just as much as I ever did. And the old way of working is I would take the most important view and make a full-size drawing of it. And then, draw lines wherever the laminations would be.

Well, there's no point in the full-size drawing anymore. Now, I go from the sketches and idea of things directly to a scale model, which really gives you a whole other kind of way of evaluating what you're doing, which I didn't have in the '60s. I could've made models in the '60s, but they wouldn't have been helpful in making the piece. They might've been helpful in making artistic judgments but there wouldn't have been any benefit in the making. Now, they're a great benefit in the making because we

Fig. 6. *Veiled in a Dream*, 2014. Cast bronze, 69¼ x 78 x 43 in. (175.9 x 198.1 x 109.2 cm). Courtesy of Margaret and Daniel S. Loeb, New York, NY.

It is very important to underscore that these digital processes do not replace the handwork in his furniture making, but rather expand his capability to realize construction elements such as complicated undercuts that could not have been achieved otherwise.

In summary, the sequence of production in Wendell Castle's previous process started with a sketch or drawing that would be refined and projected onto a wall in full scale using an overhead projector. Castle would envision the form in his mind and then predict where the slices should occur in relation to the overall form, taking into consideration the stress on the object when in use, such as a cantilevered chair seat. From this planning, he would determine the successive horizontal cross sections and translate them onto paper that served as templates for cutting out layers of one-inch-thick sheets of wood using a band saw. He then glued and stacked these layers to create the rough furniture form. To minimize warping of the wood and to make the piece lighter in weight, he also cut away the interior of each sheet of wood so that the volumetric forms were hollow when complete. A small allowance of wood on the outside surface of the cross section allowed for an overall surface treatment, whether sanded smooth or carved with texture, and finished.

Castle's process today still begins with sketches and drawings, from which he carves a small model by hand from a block of hard foam. The model is then 3D-scanned, and the 3D model is further refined using computer software. The cross sections are determined on the 3D model, with that information sent to an architectural plotter that prints out the cross sections on paper in full scale. These serve as the templates for the band sawing, gluing, and clamping by Castle or his assistants. When completely dry, a six-axis CNC milling robot finishes the exterior, and sometimes completes the interior in the case of cabinets, using a series of finer and finer drills and other tool bits, after which the piece receives surface treatment by a studio assistant. Castle commented:

In retrospect, Wendell Castle's unique method of stack lamination from the 1960s—in which individual layers of wood are built up to create a three-dimensional form—may be viewed as a type of proto-additive fabrication or 3D printing. The built-up layers of wood in stack lamination are not unlike the layers of laser-cut, stacked paper or cardboard in laminated object manufacturing, with Castle's imagination serving as the 3D model and the CAD software, and his hands and workshop tools as the 3D printer. But with the incorporation of the new digital technologies into his individual practice, Castle has streamlined the process, with the added benefits of faster production and more complicated forms of a greater scale. By linking the past with the present through a continuing balance between creativity and invention, Castle blends craftsmanship with emerging digital technologies to create highly sculptural works, yet they remain quintessentially Wendell Castle, the master.

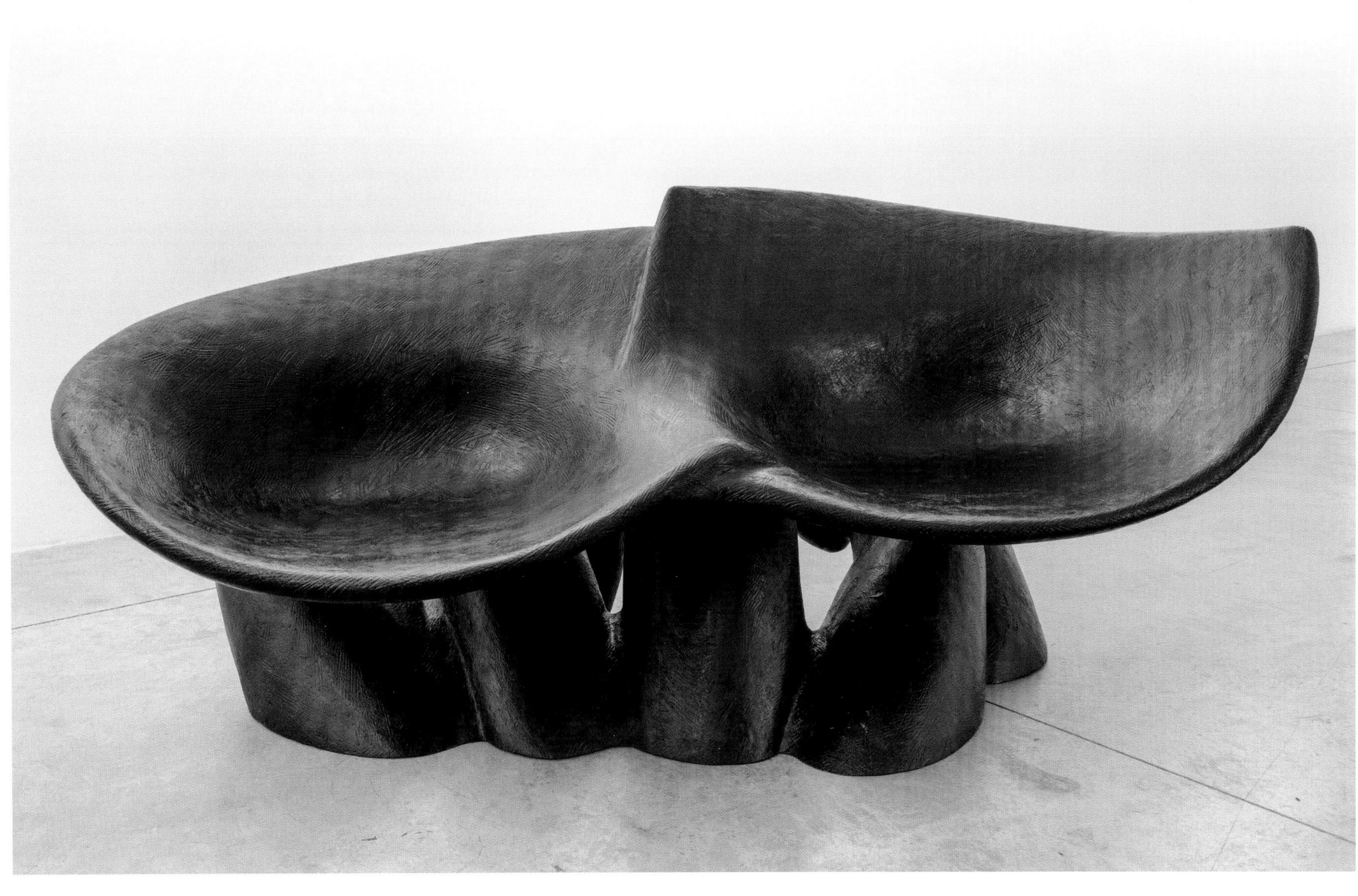

Wendell Castle: Here and There, Then and Now

LOWERY STOKES SIMS

THIS INTERVIEW WAS CONDUCTED IN SCOTTSVILLE, NEW YORK, on March 24, 2015 at the Scottsville Diner and at Wendell Castle's studio.

LOWERY STOKES SIMS: It is interesting that you are showing works in bronze in the exhibition being organized by Ron Labaco at the Museum of Arts and Design. Is this the first time you've worked in bronze?

WENDELL CASTLE: I worked in bronze in college at the University of Kansas. It was one of the first schools to have a really professional faculty for casting and facilities for casting several hundred pounds of bronze. But then when I got out of school, I couldn't afford it anymore, so I didn't do any casting. During the time that I was with the Peter Joseph Gallery I did a little bit, but now we're doing a lot more, because we're working with Carpenters Workshop Gallery in London, which works with a foundry located outside of Paris.

LOWERY: Did you also weld metal or carve?

WENDELL: Yes. I did welding and some carving. Although they didn't especially focus on woodworking at the University of Kansas, they had a shop where you could do a bit of both, which I did.

LOWERY: Was it just that wood wasn't considered serious sculptural material?

WENDELL: No, but I don't think the instructor thought much about fabricating. He thought about just carving wood, like Henry Moore, working more with a log. I didn't like that approach. Logs seemed to me to be awkward, and they're green, and they're going to crack. So I didn't really like carving out of logs. So I began to fabricate. I like building things.

LOWERY: Is that where the stack-lamination process came in?

WENDELL: Yes, it grew out of that.

LOWERY: Is it true that you were attracted to that technique because you saw an article explaining how to make duck decoys?

WENDELL: Well, indirectly. When I was a kid, I saw a step-by-step explanation, "how-to-build-a-decoy-duck" article in a 1945 issue of *Deltacraft* magazine. It showed how wooden decoys are made and how they cut the shapes out and glue them together, and then how they carve the rest of it. It was interesting that they weren't made out of a solid piece of wood. And I remembered that. I thought that was pretty cool. I really liked the idea that you could glue pieces of wood together and get shapes.

Fig. 7. *Impulse Gatherer*, 2013. Cast bronze, 31½ x 68⁹/₁₀ x 42 in. (80 x 175 x 107 cm). Courtesy of the artist, Friedman Benda, New York, NY, and Carpenters Workshop Gallery, London and Paris.

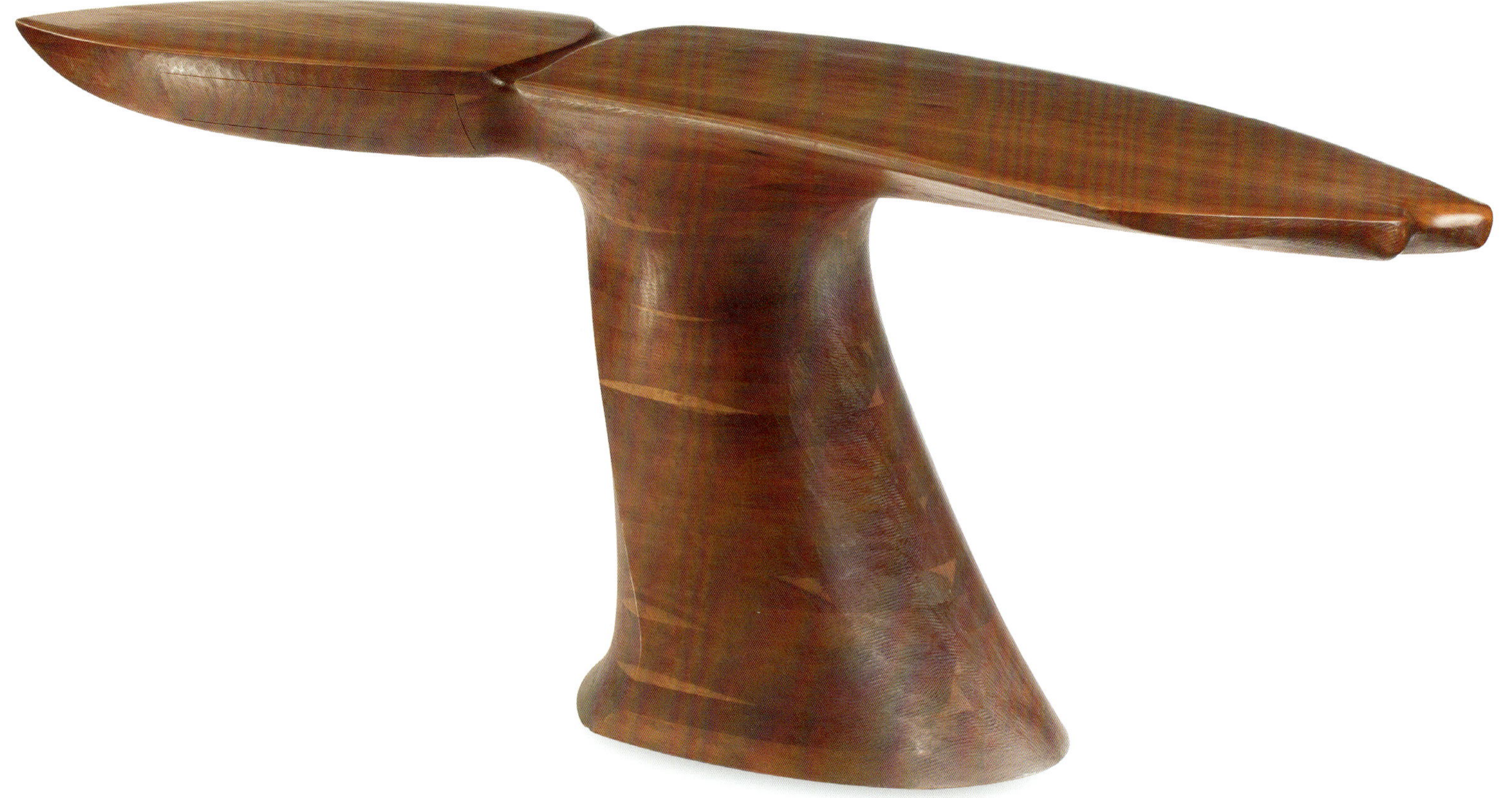

LOWERY: So you thought you could have control over the action of the wood through the technique of stack lamination.

WENDELL: You have a lot more control. You could just build that perfect log by gluing the wood together. But it's really concentrating on the process of how lamination allows you to do these things. Before we started using computer technology, I had to imagine the cross sections for the piece in order to precut them. But now with digital technology, we can go much farther in cross sections that are really complex, and can do it with ease.

LOWERY: When you arrived at the Rochester Institute of Technology [RIT] to teach, that was about the same time that you were segueing into furniture. What was the reaction of your fellow faculty members? Was that considered a usual path to take? Did they make hard-and-fast distinctions between sculpture and craft?

WENDELL: No, not very much. When I came to RIT, I really did not intend to be a furniture maker. I intended to continue with my sculpture and I did for the first year; but then gradually, I found myself around furniture and I began to see the field that exists. I didn't know about the field, I didn't know that group existed: Wharton Esherick, Sam Maloof, Art Carpenter, and George Nakashima. But then when I saw them and their work, I thought, this is an awfully small group, and I really think I'm capable of jumping right in there and becoming right up there at the same level of all those people.

LOWERY: So it was a strategic decision on your part?

Fig. 8. *Desk*, 1968. Cherry, 29 ¾ x 74 ¼ x 28 in. (75.6 x 188.6 x 71.1 cm). Courtesy of Wendell Castle and Nancy Jurs.

WENDELL: Yes, like anybody who's trying to succeed in some field. I could see that the sculpture field was very overcrowded. The furniture field was empty. And I thought, well, here's a chance. If I can do something unique in this field, I ought to be able to be recognized very soon. And I was.

LOWERY: That's very interesting. Now Richard Artschwager took the opposite path to you, at about the same time.

WENDELL: Yes, he did.

LOWERY: He started out as a furniture maker, and then he had a catastrophic fire, and then he started making sculpture. But I've always been interested in the way that his sculpture can refer to furniture forms.

WENDELL: Yes, it does.

LOWERY: So, do you think that your respective career moves led to the art world regarding his work and career differently from how it regarded yours?

WENDELL: I think it did. But I think he brought something from the furniture making into fine arts, and I brought something from sculpture into furniture making, and I think they both, in a sense, are unique because of that.

LOWERY: With regard to your work: writers have attributed your more organic forms to the influence of artists such as Henry Moore and Constantin Brâncuşi, and specifically Jean Arp and Joan Miró. They were known for their biomorphic shapes, so was it your intention to adopt that vocabulary?

WENDELL: It was partly biological because I thought of them as organic forms that would grow and that would be a specific kind of style. Some writers have suggested that this reflects the influence of my

Fig. 9. *Table*, 1969. Walnut; table: 20 x 30 x 31 in. (50.8 x 76.2 x 78.7 cm); sculpture: 16 x 34 x 13 in. (40.6 x 86.3 x 33 cm). Courtesy of Margaret and Daniel S. Loeb, New York, NY.

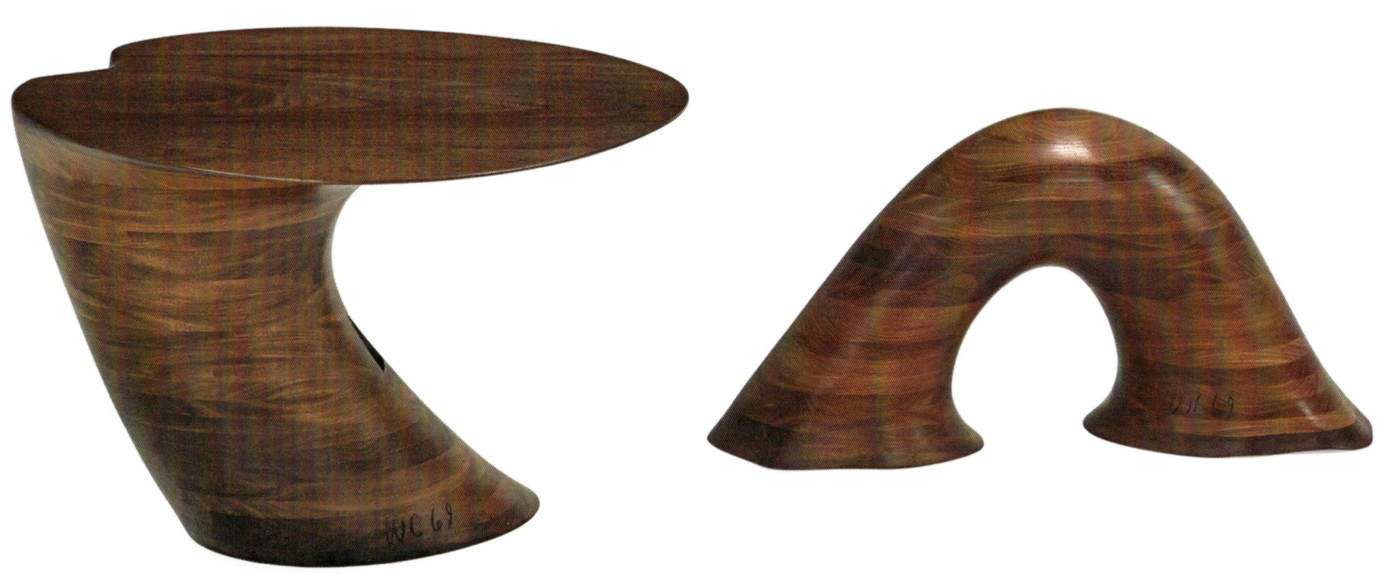

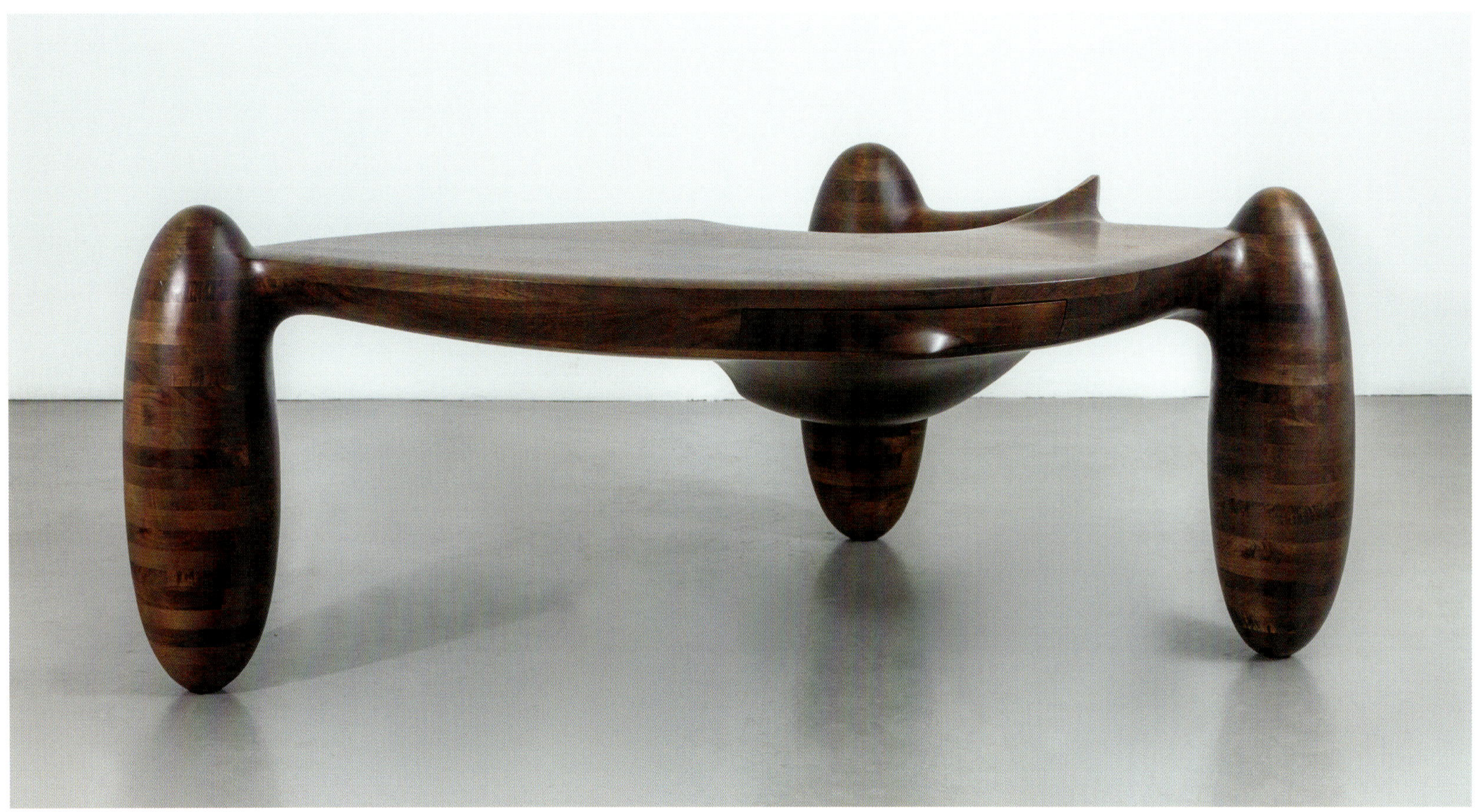

Fig. 10. *Three-Legged Desk*, 1969. Walnut, 30½ x 72 x 56 in. (77.5 x 182.9 x 142.2 cm). Courtesy of Margaret and Daniel S. Loeb, New York, NY.

upbringing in the Midwest around a lot of farms. But a lot of the shapes come out of my drawing. Sometimes I just draw shapes, and they're not anything, and if they look kind of interesting, then maybe I try to make them into something. But I'm usually, when I'm drawing, at least in a doodle stage or earlier, I don't know whether it's a table, a chair, a desk, or a cabinet. Then I see what it might be.

LOWERY: I was trying to relate this to your observation that you wanted to eliminate the standard legs on a chair, and how you conceived a central core from which forms could fan out in a growth pattern.

WENDELL: I think that came more from my idea that it is difficult to make legs as sculpture but easier to make a base for sculpture. So while some pieces have legs, the pieces that I think are important really don't have legs in the traditional sense. They have a base and I just think there's more opportunity there for sculpture.

This can be seen in works that have the support off to the side. I think it gives them some drama, at least more drama than when the pedestal's right under it. But that seems logical, and I'm trying to be illogical. This was also to distance my work from traditional furniture and to have people see it as sculpture.

LOWERY: Yes. Well, it's interesting there still is that bifurcation, because even if a sculptor chooses to do furniture as a sideline—like Scott Burton or Donald Judd—there seems also to be a distinction made between the two aspects of their work. To pursue this matter further, what I was interested in is how your career has migrated from "sculpture" to "furniture," maybe "craft," but I think people think of you more as a "designer" now.

WENDELL: Well if I had to choose, "craft" would be my last choice. Up until, say, a year or two ago, I think I felt very comfortable that people thought of me as a designer. But given what's happened with my work in the last two years, it's not clearly design anymore. I mean, there are things about it that are unlike design, and they're not really—they're totally impractical, make no sense.

LOWERY: Maybe you're coming back to being a sculptor.

WENDELL: So, yes, that's what I'm getting at. Even though my work has an element that is a seat or a desk, it also has other elements that have nothing to do with any function. But it's a set. They go together.

LOWERY: Was that your idea, to feature recent interpretations of earlier work in the MAD exhibition?

WENDELL: Indirectly, because I talked about that; but then Ron Labaco came up with the idea of remastered and the specifics of it. The purpose of the show is to feature early work, which I would like to think was groundbreaking and introduced techniques that were not typically used for furniture, and then to skip to what I am doing now, and show how technology has changed where I've gotten to now. Without technology, it would be difficult to be doing these things I'm doing now. Technology makes it practical, if that's possible, to be practical.

LOWERY: I wanted to chat about the fiberglass pieces and I remember when I first saw them, I thought they were so futuristic. I was curious about what led you to look at fiberglass and create those kinds of forms.

WENDELL: Well, two things happened. One is, I became a little tired that everything I made was brown. And the second was that I subscribed to *Domus* magazine where I saw what the Italians were doing at that time. They were doing some pretty slick-looking things and color was everywhere. I thought, gee, that's great. I like that color. And the first thing I did was actually just paint some of my wooden pieces, which was not a very good idea because wood moves and paint doesn't.

And then I thought, well, I'll put fiberglass over the wood, and that was kind of a real pain in the ass to do, but it worked a little better. And then I thought it would be even better just to make them out of fiberglass, and then you could get colored fiberglass.

So, we're not doing too much fiberglass now, but I'm going to do one new fiberglass piece, and the idea is to show a shelf from the 1969 *Cloud* series along with a new version that has the vocabulary that I'm now using and is also in fiberglass.

LOWERY: How is the vocabulary you're using now different from that you used earlier in your career?

WENDELL: Well, the early work was certainly very organic, and even occasionally based upon actually observing a bone or a shell. I'm not really looking at any bones or shells now, but the new work reflects those shapes and their kind of organic growth.

Part of the vocabulary that really started several years ago came from looking at a seed form as an ellipsoid. But an ellipsoid in itself isn't so interesting. It is kind of a football shape (my wife Nancy calls them torpedoes). But if you merge one into another, then the forms get pretty interesting. Then I started making them a little pointier and I stretched their ends out and so in the recent work, they don't look like seeds anymore but they do look like something growing.

LOWERY: But you know, Wendell, when I look at pictures of the works in the exhibition, particularly of the new things, I think about how they would function in a specific environment. I also find that to me they can be slightly disconcerting—almost a little scary. I think of science fiction imagery from the 1950s that involve pods taking over human bodies.

WENDELL: I would prefer to think that I'm dealing with discomfort. I think this can mean two things: the actual sitting in the chair is uncomfortable, and if you look at the piece you feel uncomfortable because you're not exactly sure what you're dealing with, particularly if you should approach it from the side or back. You don't have, really, any idea what that is. And I like that idea that it's not immediately giving itself away to what it is.

I don't think they're actually threatening. But, you may feel uncomfortable around them, particularly the bigger ones. If you walk up to something where you have to look up at it, that's different from walking up to normal furniture where you look down.

LOWERY: So it's cultivating the unexpected.

WENDELL: Yes.

LOWERY: Speaking of bigger pieces, it is interesting to look at the maquettes you have prepared for more environmental works. I remember seeing *A New Environment* at Friedman Benda Gallery in 2013. I think I have a picture of you climbing up to the pod form on top and then down the stairs. The environments really interest me in many ways because I wondered if you thought about them in terms of sort of nomadic architecture since their shapes look like teepees or huts.

WENDELL: Yes, this new one particularly, more than the others, I think. But this is the fifth design I've made for an environment and the first two I designed were really big. A half-a-dozen people could be in them. But then I realized how unpractical that is and how much it was going to cost me to make it. Then I made one that was kind of like a car. But—even though I kind of liked it—that didn't seem to have anything to do with the vocabulary I'm working with.

LOWERY: So what's your motivation for making an environment for a group of people? Obviously you're not just making something for people to sit in; you're also interested in creating situations where they can relate to each other in specific ways.

WENDELL: What I thought about is: people get inside cars, but it's not practical to put a car in your house (although some people have). So I thought they could relate to personal privacy. Initially, I thought about just for one person to get in there just to contemplate. *Environment for Contemplation* (1969–1970, plate 25) was in the exhibition *Contemplation Environments* at the Museum of Contemporary Crafts. Afterward, it was in my living room here and I kind of enjoyed it because it was a great place to go in and take a nap. You'd close the door and it was not completely dark, but darkish. And it was kind of comforting. This new one is similar to that but there is enough room for a second person.

What makes some of the bigger new works different is that the forms would be impossible without the Robot. So essentially we would not have been able to build them back in the 1960s. You just couldn't have done it. Or it would have been a lifetime project if you tried.

Also, we can make the works more accessible because with computer technology we have the ability to construct the pieces so that they can come apart and we can get into different spaces more easily. That involves a complex cut of curves, and with robotics you can get a perfect cut.

LOWERY: So in many ways, technology is offering you a way to do things that you could only dream about before. Has this been the case at different phases of your career, that some technology came along and allowed you to do something that you couldn't have before? Or is this particular moment a sort of watershed for you in terms of jumping to the next phase of your work?

WENDELL: There were no real advances in technology until about ten years ago, and I didn't get into it until about five years ago. I knew about it, because they were doing it in Europe earlier than here. A good example is Jeroen Verhoeven's *Cinderella Table*. That was done with a CNC technique—what

Fig. 11. *Light of Darkness*, 2012. (Installation view, *Wendell Castle: A New Environment*, Friedman Benda, New York, NY, January 10–February 9, 2013.) Stained ash and lighting element, 72¾ x 72¾ x 75¼ in. (184.8 x 184.8 x 191.1 cm). Courtesy of Friedman Benda, New York, NY.

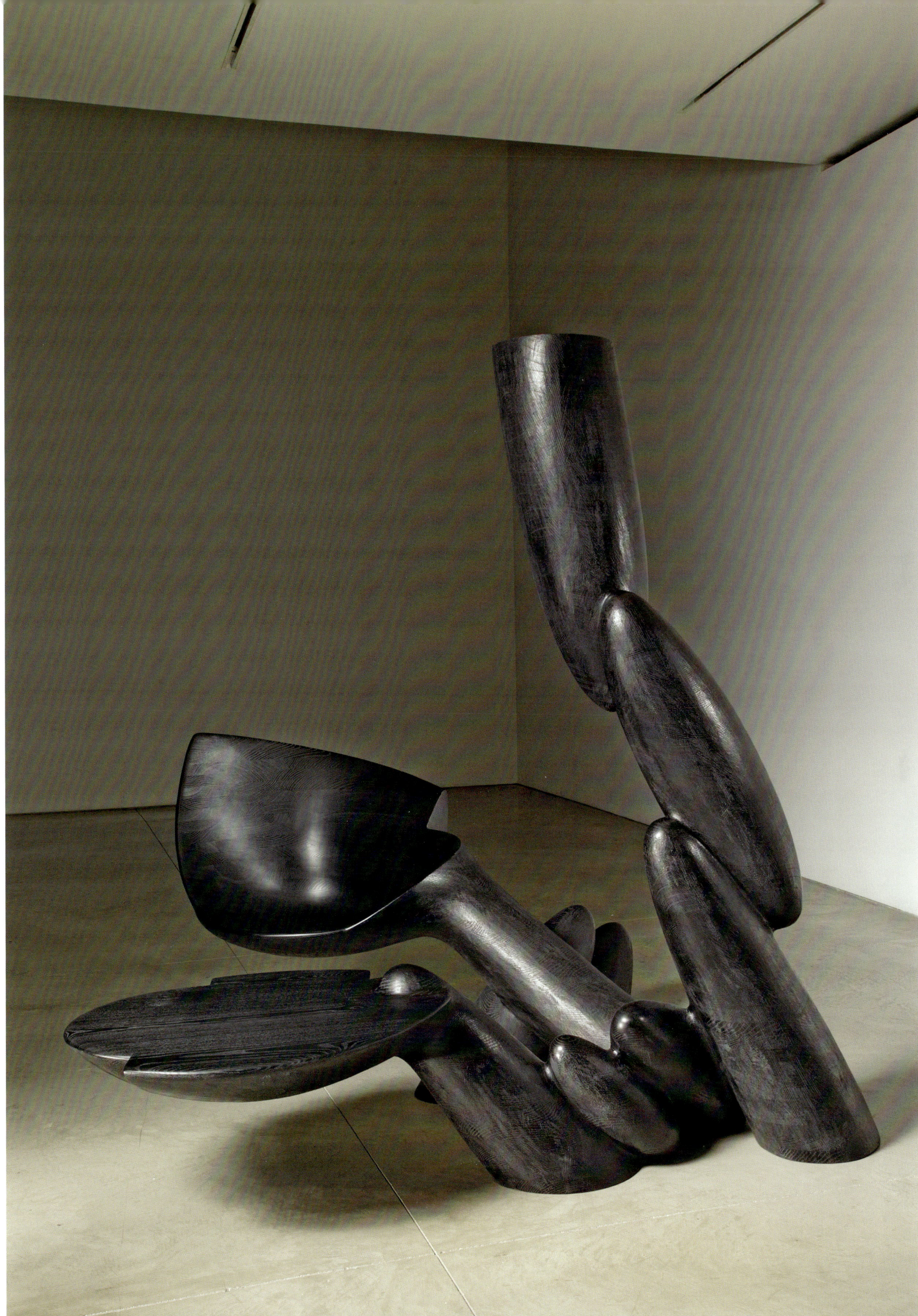

we do here. The table had to be made in pieces or you wouldn't have been able to achieve the intricate elbow curves in the forms. And that is a real breakthrough, the fact that you can reach things that you couldn't have reached even with hand tools. The most amazing work I've seen along these lines is Paul McCarthy's *White Snow Bookends* (2013).

LOWERY: It is interesting, though, that artists are sometimes reluctant to reveal the fact that they use digital media even though it was obvious that they were.

WENDELL: Yes. But this technique seldom makes a whole piece. But it can do the parts that you could not have done otherwise. If you had a carving contest, and everything could be reached, it would be about a tie between a good carver and the Robot. So it's not necessarily quicker. It can just do things that you couldn't do, in the sense of accuracy, too.

LOWERY: What do you like best about working with technology?

WENDELL: I enjoy the element of risk, the uncertainty of whether it will come out alright, the uncertainty of where it might end up, and I'm comfortable with those things, and I'm uncomfortable with the opposite situation. The opposite would be that you make something and a lot of people like it, so you make some more. That, to me, is boring. You know, I wouldn't even be making these editions today, which are only in eight, if we didn't have the Robot, so I wouldn't have to do it. I only had to do one.

LOWERY: Right. So you don't have to make something over and over again.

WENDELL: I mean, I could go back and make that original music stand and sell them like crazy. But I'm not going to do that. That wouldn't be any fun. And I have fun.

LOWERY: And that certainly makes you different from the average furniture maker, too.

WENDELL: Yes. I'm the opposite. Most would find a good, saleable thing and make a bunch of them. In fact, all they could sell. But it was most evident at some time—I mean, I don't think I stopped making the stack laminations for that reason, because they were all different anyway; but I remember that when I did some of the *trompe l'oeil* pieces, at first they didn't sell at all, and then they started to sell well, and then I decided that's the time to stop. So that was the end of that. I wasn't going to keep turning those out.

LOWERY: Yes, I think that's always a conundrum any artist faces: Do you keep doing the same thing because you know you can make money?

WENDELL: Right now, for example, there are several works in the studio that are already finished. But, if I hadn't already finished them, I'd be changing them right now. So sometimes it's good just to make it quick before you can change your mind.

LOWERY: But you don't think that the use of the computer might seduce you into making more. It would certainly facilitate that….

WENDELL: It does. It does, and particularly on a piece where it can do every aspect of it, one hundred percent. Like that little table in the studio (plate 31). But on most pieces, you could do entirely using technology, but there's really not any point to it, because you can do it just as well by hand. …

LOWERY: So you're saying that you prefer to make unique pieces rather than editions? Are you working now mostly on commissioned work or on pieces that you want to create?

WENDELL: I'm not really doing any commissions these days. I haven't had one in several years. These are all just pieces that I am making and hopefully then will find a home, which, so far, has, you know, been working out okay.

The last commission I did, which is a couple of years ago now, is *Unicorn Family*, the cast-iron chairs that are in front of the Memorial Art Gallery, as part of the installations at the Centennial Sculpture Park. You know, that commission came from the local museum, and the director and I are good friends, and that was kind of—I could do whatever I wanted. So that kind of commission I would accept.

LOWERY: With all this involvement with technology, do you think people still have that kind of romantic notion they've always had about woodworking furniture and the involvement of the hand?

WENDELL: Mm-hmm. I mean, to me it's silly. If you think of somebody like Edward Barnsley—who was carrying on the arts and crafts traditions of his father—he didn't even have electricity until in the 1960s or 1970s, when he was an old man. He had a power table saw that he ran with a gasoline engine and did everything by hand. He thought that was the right way to make things and he made beautiful things very well. But he was living in another century. It made no sense. And I suppose the first time a band saw had been around—and they've been around for 100 years—probably people thought, what's this world coming to, you know? We're not making anything by hand anymore. I can't see any reasons that, if a tool was available, why not use it? Using a chainsaw as opposed to a chisel doesn't necessarily make it better, but it makes it a lot more practical.

LOWERY: I wanted to go back to the new lamp, *High Hopes* [2015, plate 12], that we saw in the studio, which allows one to control the colors and patterns of the lights with an iPad. How did that idea come about?

WENDELL: Well, the one thing that's interesting about lamps is that they can be totally sculptural. They don't immediately give their function away. Even the older lamp that they're going to borrow for the MAD exhibition [*Serpentine Floor Lamp*, 1965–1967, plate 11] is more sculptural than functional looking because of its size, and the way it's shaped. Although you might figure it out because it can be outfitted with a more normal shade. But that's the reason that lamps are interesting, and I've done some others with LED lights in the side, although it's not practical to do them. They're harder to sell. Chairs . . . you can always sell chairs.

LOWERY: So, where to next?

WENDELL: I've thought about printing some furniture. I mean, our robot could be adapted to do it. You just have to set it up so that it has the ability to extrude molten plastic that cools at room temperature. I would print gigantic things that way. But the material isn't so nice. I mean, wood is really nice. You know, you want to put your hand on it and it's such a nice material. The plastics and other materials that are used in 3D printing are a little bit rough. But boy, you can do some crazy stuff, though. But I haven't gone there.

LOWERY: But who knows?

WENDELL: But to me, bronze and wood are the two best materials to make furniture out of.

LOWERY: Not fiberglass?

WENDELL: No, fiberglass isn't as good. It lets you do it much cheaper. The wood and the bronze are not going to be cheap, where the fiberglass could be, particularly the way I did it in the 1960s. It was cheap because I worked on designs that would come out of the mold complete. I'm not doing that now. I wonder if we should see if that piece has been put together in the studio.

LOWERY: *Let's go.*

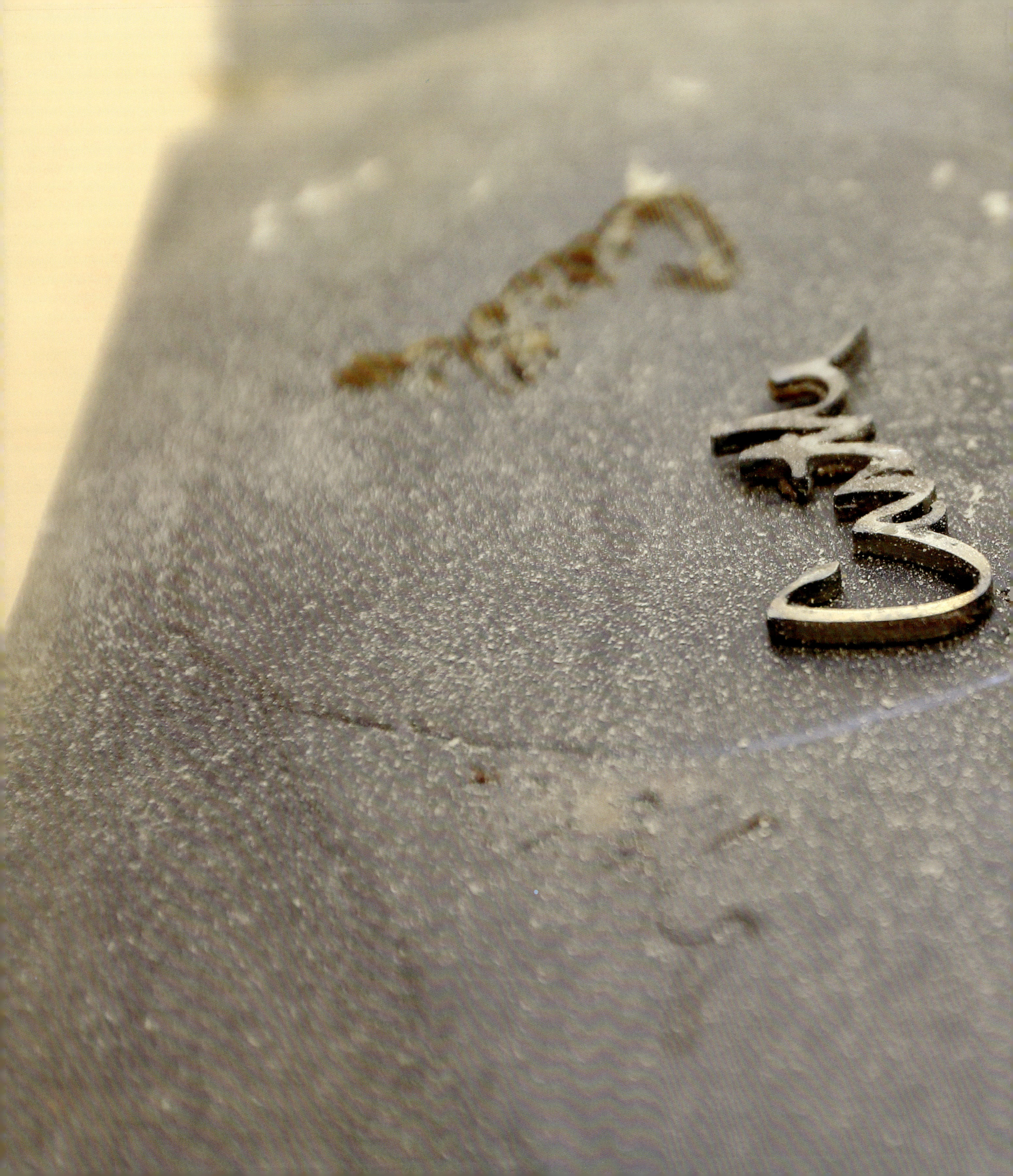

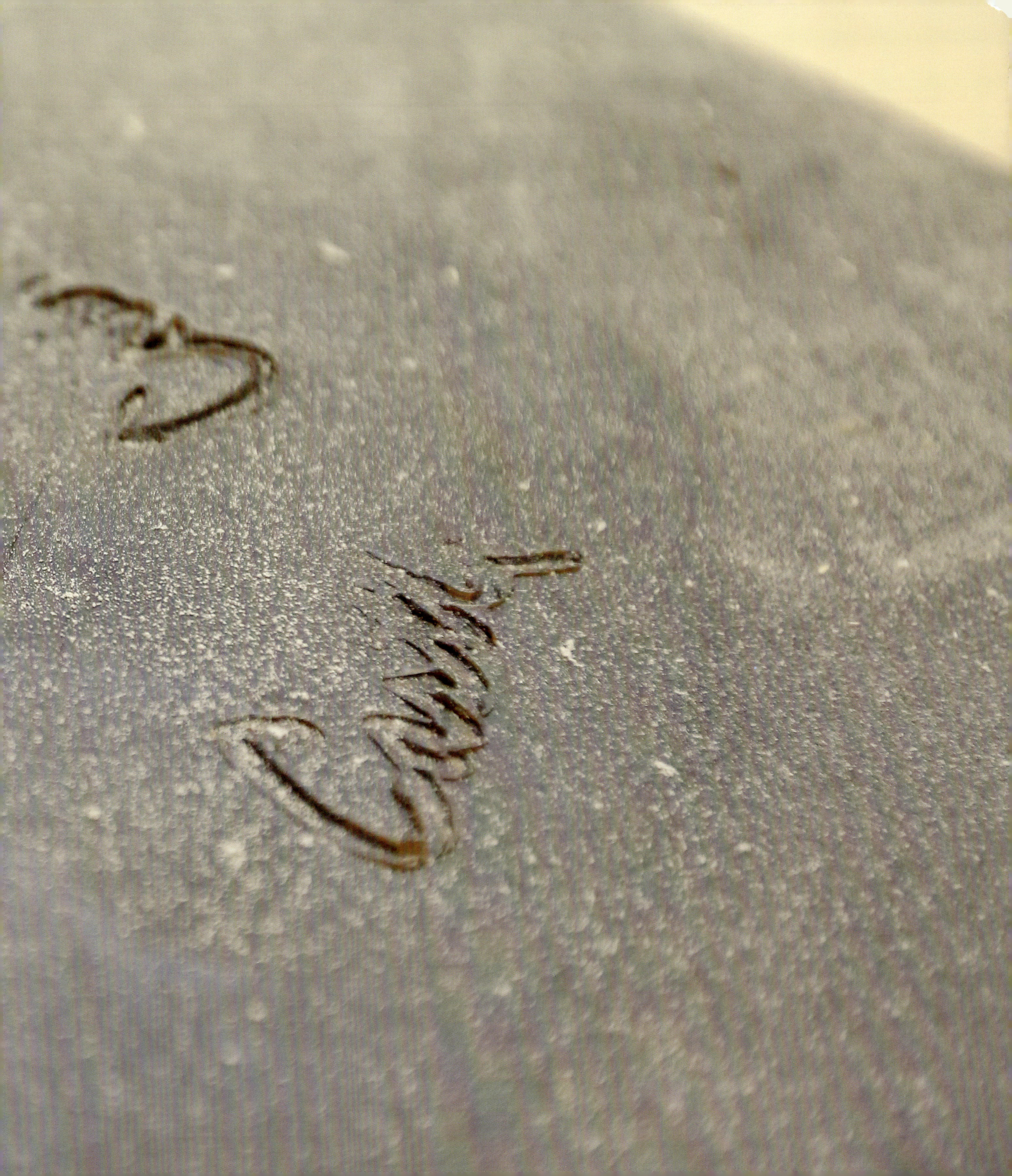

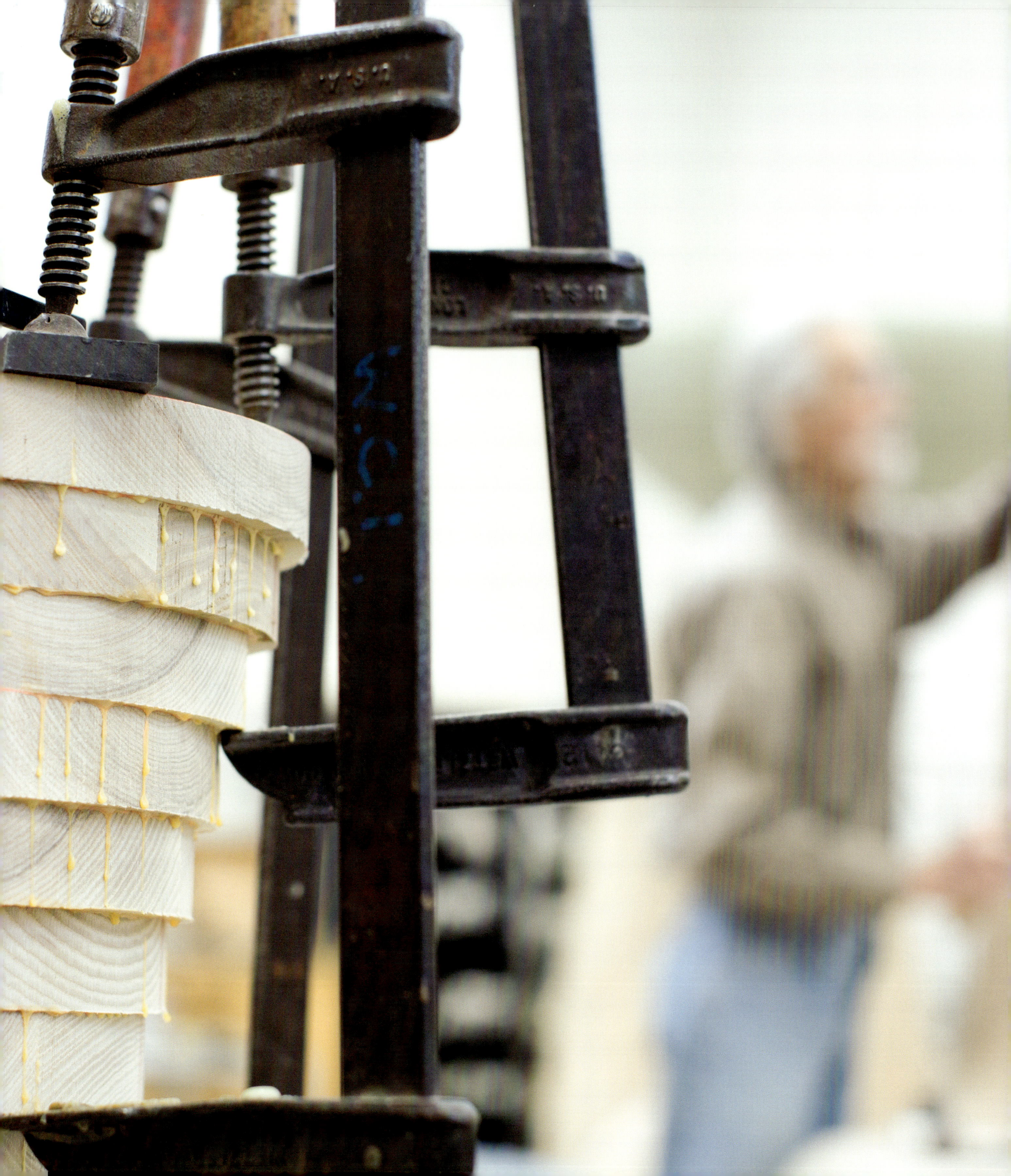

Artworks

SAMANTHA De TILLIO

WHEN STUDYING THE WORK OF WENDELL CASTLE with an eye toward process, an interesting evolution of forms emerges. His disregard for traditional woodworking techniques and insistence on sculptural methodologies has resulted in the creation of a body of work that is uniquely biomorphic and aesthetically driven. Additionally, his utilization of reductive carving methods and his exploration of volume has created interesting comparisons to more traditionally labeled fine artists, such as Henry Moore (1898–1986) and Alberto Giacometti (1901–1966), proving his ability to walk the divide between art, craft, and design.[1]

Wendell Castle Remastered illustrates Castle's coexistence in the worlds of both sculpture and furniture with examples that drive home the many breakthrough moments that result from the progression of his process, including *Stool* (plate 3), *Chair with Table* (plate 7), *Squid Chair No. 1* (plate 17), *Dining Table* (plate 14), and *Long Night* (plate 5). Additionally, the exhibition brings to light the thread that weaves its way through Castle's career, connecting it to the Museum of Arts and Design through many exhibitions from 1962 to the present. This exhibition delves into Castle's newest take on process, his exploration of digital technology.

NOTE TO THE READER: Much of the artwork has been created specifically for this exhibition. When works were not completed in time to be photographed for this catalogue, an image of the urethane-foam model, digital rendering, or drawing has been supplied to represent the finished piece.

1. Martin Eidelberg, ed., *Design 1935–1965: What Modern Was* (New York: Harry N. Abrams, Inc., in association with The Museum of Decorative Arts, Montreal, 1991), 287; Alastair Gordon, *Wendell Castle Wandering Forms—Works from 1959–1979* (New York: Gregory R. Miller & Co. in association with the Aldrich Contemporary Art Museum, Ridgefield, CT, 2012), 44.

Walnut Sculpture, 1958–1959

During the 1950s, Castle was a student at the University of Kansas, first earning a bachelor of fine arts in industrial design and then a master of fine arts in sculpture. He took courses in metalworking and casting, and in wood carving, which he recalls was not his strongest subject at the time.[1] He took a silversmithing elective and was able to use the sculpture department's metalcasting foundry—one of the first university foundries in the country.[2]

It was while doing his graduate work that Castle began to create dynamic sculptures made from gunstock blanks sourced from a nearby factory, work aptly described as three-dimensional drawings by art critic and curator Alastair Gordon.[3] *Walnut Sculpture* is one of the strongest examples of this series. Although rooted in the fine arts, these gunstock sculptures encouraged Castle to begin experimenting with the idea of sculpture-cum-furniture, or works that were interchangeable.

1. Oral history interview with Wendell Castle, June 3–December 12, 1981, Archives of American Art, Smithsonian Institution, Washington, DC.

2. Ibid.; author's telephone interview with Wendell Castle, March 25, 2015.

3. Gordon, *Wendell Castle: Wandering Forms,* 34, 36; Emily Evans Eerdmans, ed., *Wendell Castle: A Catalogue Raisonné, 1958–2012* (New York: The Artist Book Foundation, 2015), 49.

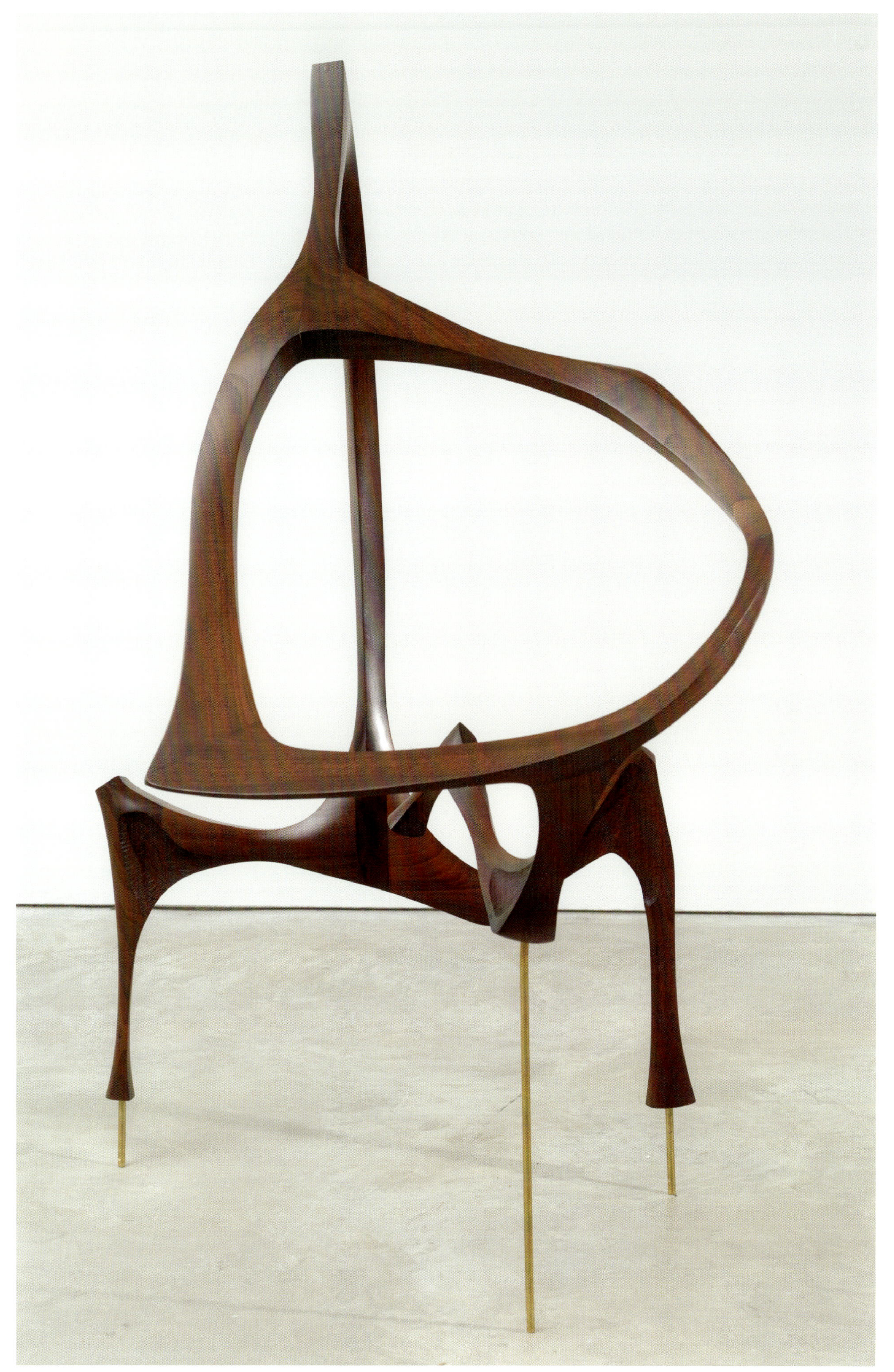

Scribe's Stool, 1961–1962

As Castle's interest in merging sculpture and furniture grew, his abstract gunstock creations matured into *Stool Sculpture* (1959) and *Scribe's Stool*.[1] Both had the same spindly quality dictated by the materials he used, and although they were functional, they were only barely so. Castle's affinity for the fine arts is evident throughout his work, and these early pieces have been compared to the sculpture and drawings of Henry Moore, Alberto Giacometti, and Franz Kafka (1883–1924).[2]

In 1960, Castle's *Stool Sculpture* was accepted into the Nelson-Atkins Museum of Art in Kansas City for its *Mid-America Exhibition*. This juried exhibition was a fine arts show and, as a result, didn't include craft works; thus, even though Castle regarded *Stool Sculpture* as furniture, he submitted it as a sculpture.[3] Shortly after Castle graduated with his MFA, he moved to New York City and entered *Scribe's Stool* in *Young Americans* (1962), a major exhibition at the Museum of Contemporary Crafts (now the Museum of Arts and Design) that showcased the results of a juried competition for craftsmen under 30, sponsored by the American Craftsmen's Council.[4] *Scribe's Stool* attracted considerable attention from the press; it was called a "mad, branchy piece of wood sculpture designed on the principle of a child's high chair," by Priscilla Chapman of the *New York Herald Tribune*.[5] *Scribe's Stool* became a pinnacle work for Castle and, in a way, launched his career. After seeing it in *Young Americans*, Harold Brennan, dean of fine and applied arts at the Rochester Institute of Technology (RIT) and director of RIT's School for American Craftsmen, asked Wendell Castle to be the new professor of furniture design, a post that provided Castle with access to state-of-the-art facilities and allowed him to grow and experiment as an artist.[6]

1. Alternate date ranges can be found for this work. Here, we have used the dating found in the newly published catalogue raisonné (Eerdmans, *Wendell Castle: A Catalogue Raisonné, 1958–2012*); however, a designed and executed date range of 1959–1962 is used by the Montreal Museum of Fine Arts, which owns this piece. See Eidelberg, ed., *Design 1935–1965: What Modern Was,* 287.

2. Eidelberg, ed., *Design 1935–1965: What Modern Was,* 287; Gordon, *Wendell Castle: Wandering Forms,* 44.

3. Eidelberg, ed., *Design 1935–1965: What Modern Was,* 287–288; Gordon, *Wendell Castle: Wandering Forms,* 36; oral history interview with Wendell Castle, June 3–December 12, 1981, Archives of American Art.

4. *Young Americans* 1962 (New York: American Craftsmen's Council in association with the Museum of Contemporary Crafts), 11, 27; Eidelberg, ed., *Design 1935–1965: What Modern Was,* 288; Gordon, *Wendell Castle: Wandering Forms,* 44; Ron Labaco telephone interview with Wendell Castle, March 5, 2014.

5. Eidelberg, ed., *Design 1935–1965: What Modern Was,* 288; Gordon, *Wendell Castle: Wandering Forms,* 44; oral history interview with Wendell Castle, June 3–December 12, 1981, Archives of American Art; Davira S. Taragin, Edward S. Cooke Jr., and Joseph Giovannini, *Furniture by Wendell Castle* (New York: Hudson Hills Press in association with the Founders Society, Detroit Institute of Arts, 1996), 20.

6. Oral history interview with Wendell Castle, June 3–December 12, 1981, Archives of American Art; Taragin et al., *Furniture by Wendell Castle,* 24; Labaco telephone interview with Castle, March 5, 2014.

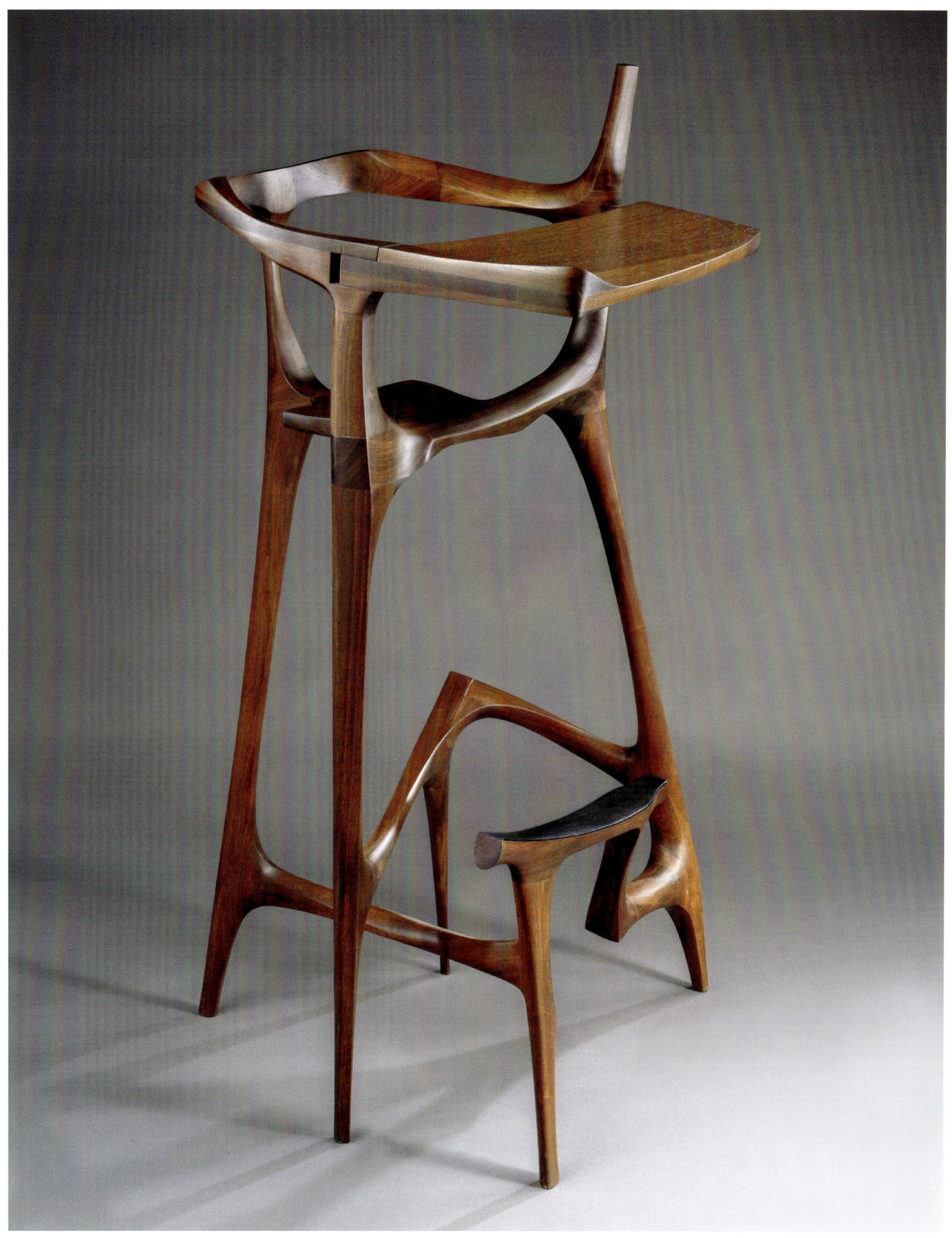

Plate 2

Stool, 1963

Stool is the first piece of furniture Castle made using stack lamination. Made during his first year as a professor at RIT, it was initially oriented with its bentwood legs reaching upward and the stack-laminated seat served as the base, but Castle realized that what was conceived as sculpture would make an interesting yet functional piece of furniture.[1] Castle had been making furniture since the late 1950s, but he primarily had used gunstock construction, bentwood, and traditional joinery. Because it was not originally meant to be functional, this stool allowed him to think about furniture from a purely sculptural standpoint, without regard to joinery, which Castle felt was a constricting way to think about furniture forms. He also freely applied his innovations in stack lamination—a technique he learned from a *Deltacraft* article that he had read when he was 13 on how to make a duck decoy—to a piece of furniture, an approach that he would develop through the 1960s and revitalize much later in his career.[2]

The summer before graduate school, Castle and a classmate were on the East Coast and made an impromptu visit to the home of artist and craftsman Wharton Esherick (1887–1970), where he very briefly glimpsed how exciting artistically made furniture could be.[3] Although he did not expect to become a furniture maker and planned to return to sculpture as soon as he could, this early period at RIT made him aware of contemporary artist furniture makers, including innovators such as Sam Maloof (1916–2009) and Arthur Espenet Carpenter (1920–2006).[4] He realized that the furniture field was in flux and studio furniture was in its infancy. Rather than start at the bottom of a well-established field such as sculpture, he could come out on top in this new style of furniture and make a name for himself.[5]

1. Gordon, *Wendell Castle: Wandering Forms*, 28; Eidelberg, ed., *Design 1935–1965*, 288; author's telephone interview with Wendell Castle, February 9, 2015.

2. Author's telephone interview with Castle, February 9, 2015; author's telephone interview with Castle, March 25, 2015; Amy Cheatle and Steven J. Jackson, "Digital Entanglements: Craft, Computation and Collaboration in Fine Arts Furniture Production" (paper presented at the 2015 Computer Supported Cooperative Work (CSCW) Conference, Vancouver, BC, February 2015), http://www.amycheatle.net/wp-content/uploads/2014/10/paper685_cscwcheatle.pdf, 5.

3. Gordon, *Wendell Castle: Wandering Forms*, 31, 34; oral history interview with Wendell Castle, June 3–December 12, 1981, Archives of American Art; Taragin et al., *Furniture by Wendell Castle*, 16.

4. Author's telephone interview with Castle, February 9, 2015; Gordon, *Wendell Castle: Wandering Forms*, 45.

5. Author's telephone interview with Castle, February 9, 2015; Lowery Stokes Sims interview with Wendell Castle, March 24, 2015, in Scottsville, NY; Gordon, *Wendell Castle: Wandering Forms*, 45.

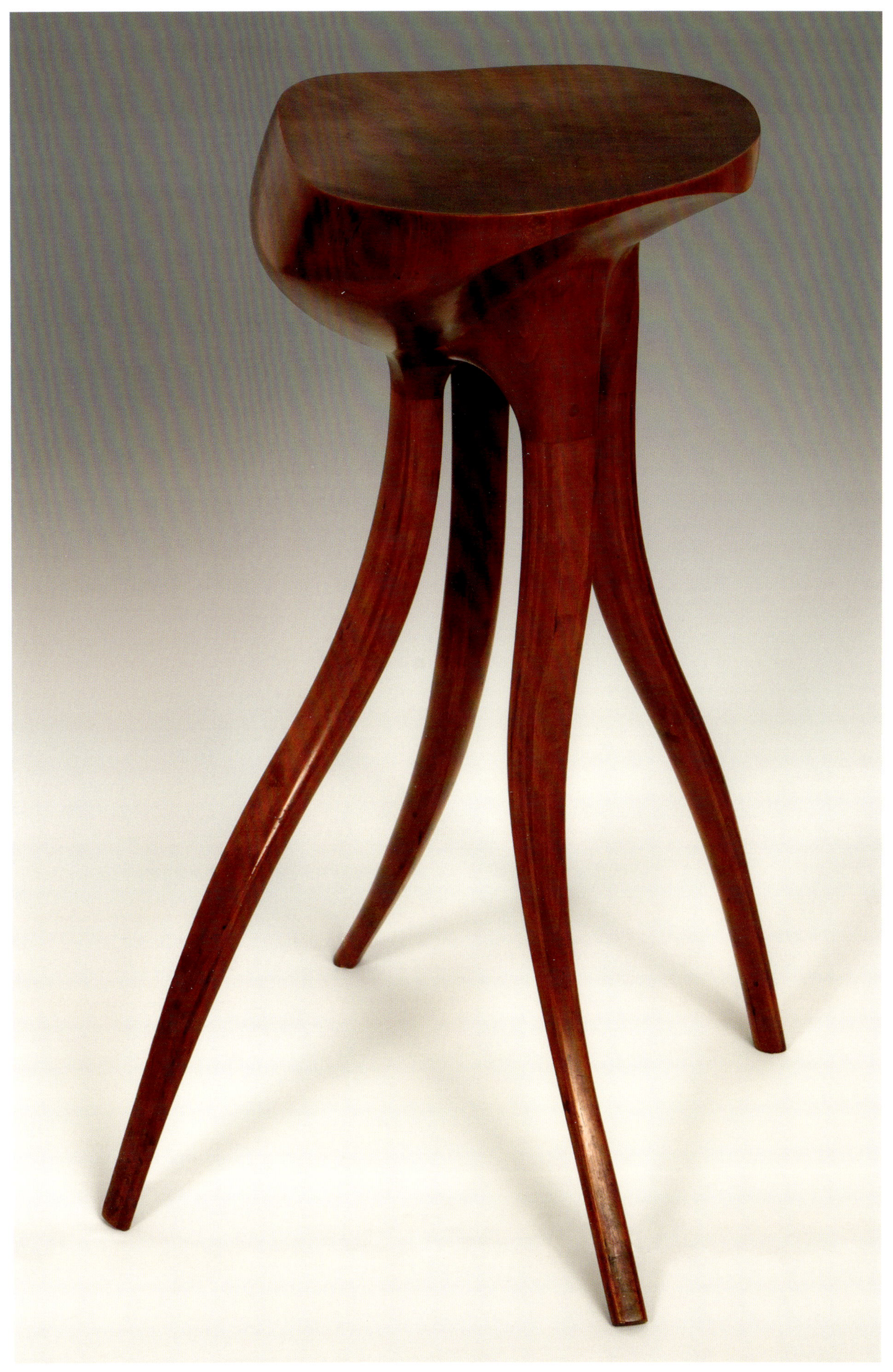

Plate 3

Blanket Chest, 1963

Although Castle had made furniture during the late 1950s and had experimented with stack lamination around this time as well, this selection of work from the 1960s marks the first combination of furniture form and technique. Prior to this, Castle was making furniture and sculpture out of gunstocks, which gave his work during the 1950s a distinctly skeletal appearance.[1] With the help of stack lamination, his work in the 1960s grew to accommodate the voluminous forms with sweeping curves that he so craved.[2] Drawing from ideas of volume found in the work of Constantin Brâncuşi (1876–1957), Hans Arp (1886–1966), and Joan Miró (1893–1983), Castle approached furniture making in the reductive method of a sculptor.[3] No work better exemplifies this transition than *Blanket Chest*. Although it was made within a year of *Stool* (plate 3), it is obvious that Castle became immensely more proficient in making stack-laminated furniture during this time, which was partially a result of his access to the extensive wood shop at RIT.[4]

Blanket Chest is the first cabinet Castle made and the first piece of case furniture with a fully finished interior, preceded only by a chest of drawers using traditional dovetail construction with bentwood legs.[5] He entered *Blanket Chest* in the *1965 Rochester-Finger Lakes Exhibition* at the Memorial Art Gallery (MAG) of the University of Rochester and was awarded the Mr. and Mrs. James Sibley Watson Purchase Prize, Jurors' Show Award.[6] With this prize, *Blanket Chest* was acquired by the museum for its permanent collection and Castle was awarded his very first solo exhibition, *Designed by Wendell Castle*, which took place at MAG in 1965.[7] Castle's tour de force, *Library Sculpture* (plates 9 and 10), was made for this exhibition and was his most ambitious work thus far, incorporating two chairs, a table, a stool, and a lamp.[8]

1. Gordon, *Wendell Castle: Wandering Forms*, 34, 36; Eerdmans, *Wendell Castle: A Catalogue Raisonné, 1958-2012*, 49.

2. Author's telephone interview with Castle, March 25, 2015.

3. Labaco telephone interview with Castle, March 5, 2014.

4. Author's telephone interview with Castle, February 9, 2015.

5. Ibid.; Eerdmans, *Wendell Castle: A Catalogue Raisonné, 1958–2012*, 76.

6. Author's telephone interview with Castle, February 9, 2015; Eerdmans, *Wendell Castle: A Catalogue Raisonné*, 76; Taragin et al., *Furniture by Wendell Castle*, 34.

7. Author's telephone interview with Castle, February 9, 2015; Gordon, *Wendell Castle: Wandering Forms*, 76; Eerdmans, *Wendell Castle: A Catalogue Raisonné*, 76, 93; Taragin et al., *Furniture by Wendell Castle*, 34.

8. Author's telephone interview with Castle, February 9, 2015; Gordon, *Wendell Castle: Wandering Forms*, 80; Eerdmans, *Wendell Castle: A Catalogue Raisonné*, 93; Taragin et al., *Furniture by Wendell Castle*, 34.

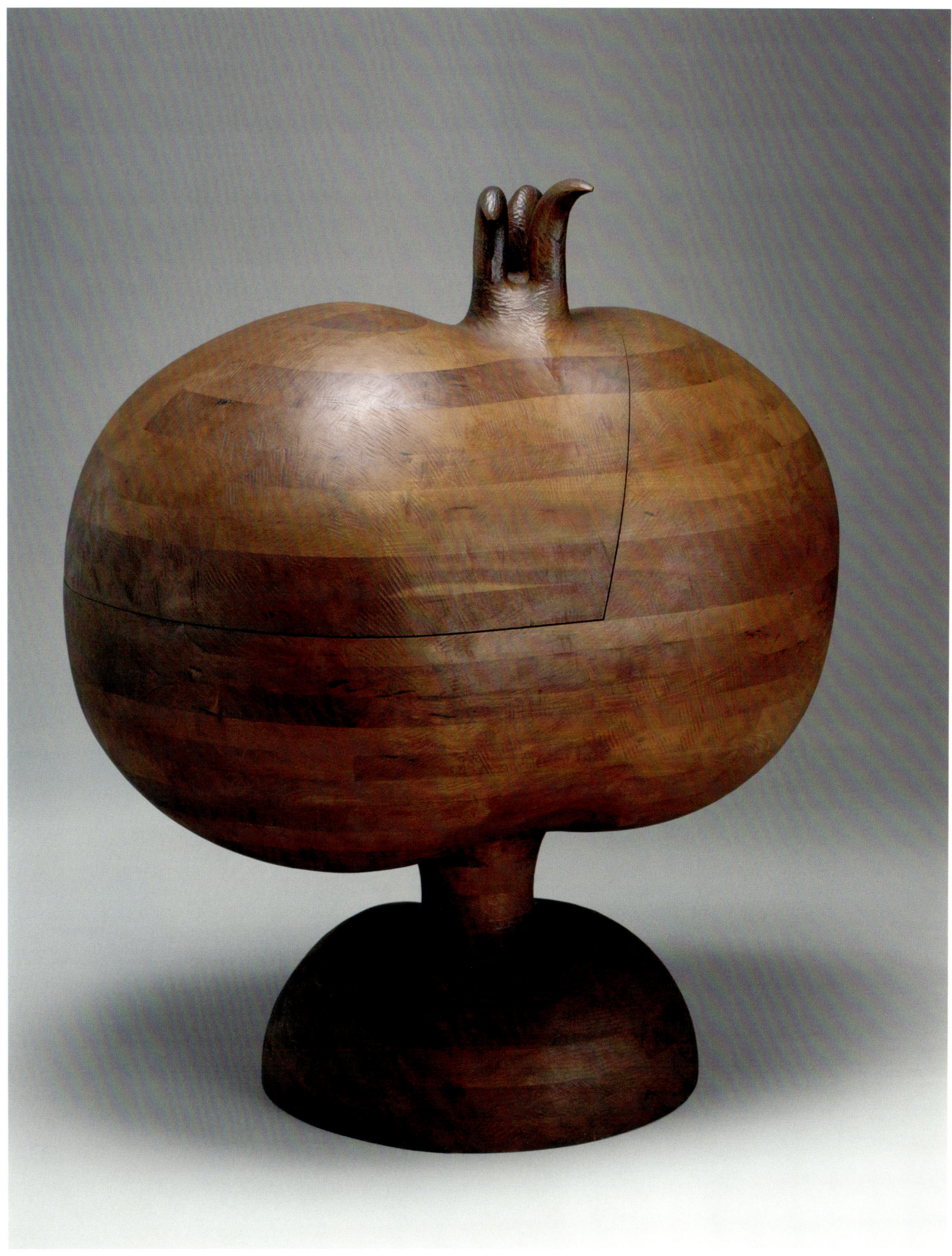

Plate 4

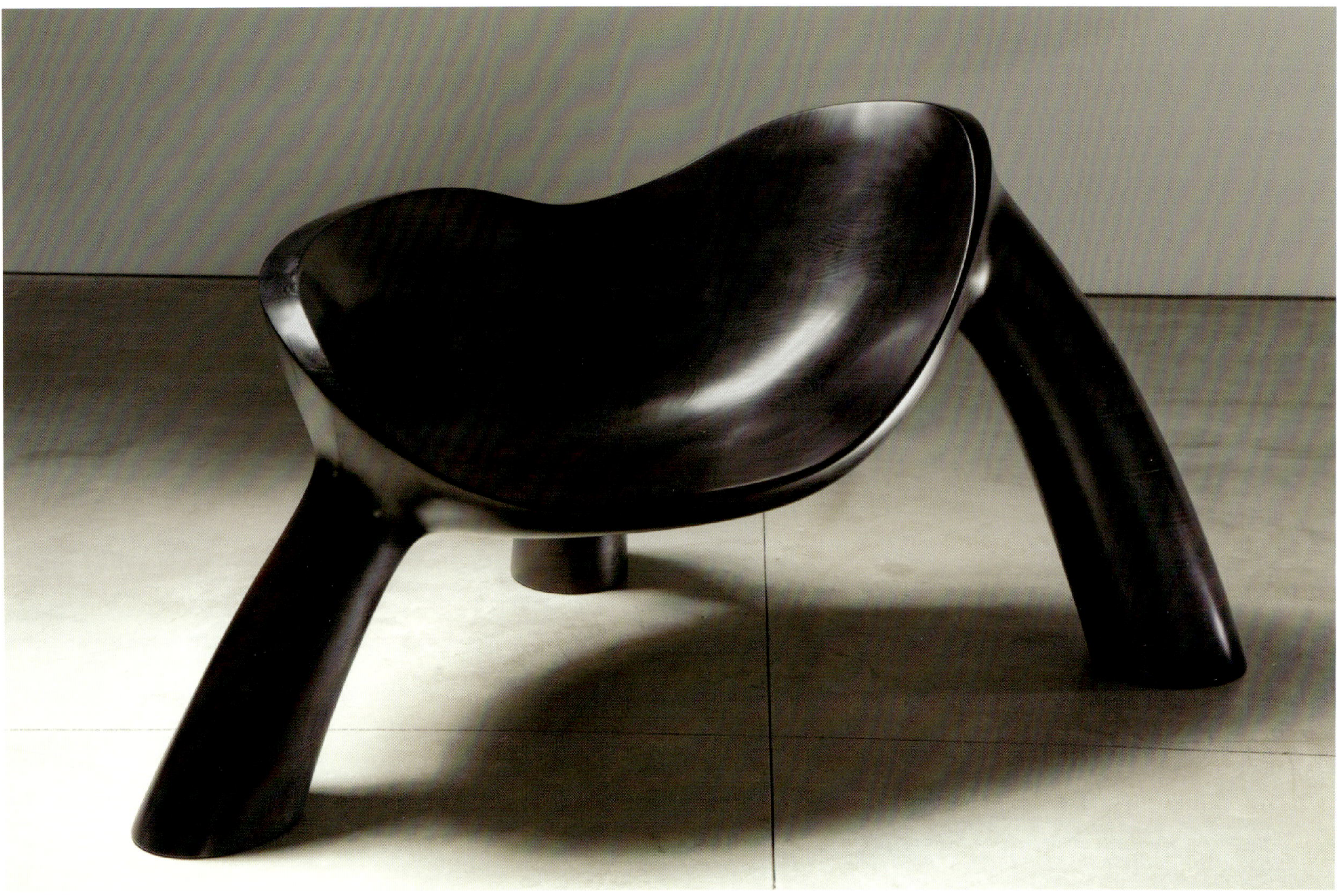

Plate 5

Long Night, 2011

After his work in the 1960s, Castle explored a variety of styles and techniques, including work in fiberglass, *trompe l'oeil*, a sculptural clock series, and traditionally crafted furniture that took the tone of Post-Modern-influenced Art Deco. The breadth of Castle's creativity clearly shows his tendency toward innovation and experimentation.

During much of the 1970s, 1980s, and 1990s, Castle's work relied on the various expertise of his staff for areas of detail where his skill did not lay, including clock mechanisms, veneering, metal-plating, and classical carving.[1] Around 2004, Castle decided it was time to abandon his increased use of his assistants' specialty skills and return to stack lamination, a technique that he perfected and one that is iconic to him as an artist.[2] Although Castle still employs assistants, he is capable of completing each step of the process himself—an aspect he feels strongly about at this point in his career.[3]

After he began laminating again, Castle became aware of a few European sculptors who were laminating in plywood; they were using a CNC (computer numerical control) machine to assist their work. He was interested in how this CNC machine could be applied to his own work and, in the late 2000s, he set out to acquire one.[4] *Long Night* is the first mature work made into an edition using this new machine, affectionately dubbed the Robot, or Mr. Chips, by the studio.

1. In the 1970s, when Castle explored more traditional wood-working techniques and elaborate veneers, he was assisted by Donald Sottile, who had those particular skills. During the 1980s, William Sloane designed and fashioned much of the hardware and mechanisms for Castle's clock series, Greg Bloomfield was brought into the shop because of his metalworking expertise, and an academically trained French carver was hired to execute several of the *trompe l'oeil* works—eventually training Castle and Sottile so that they could be self-sufficient. See Taragin et al., *Furniture by Wendell Castle*, 52, 54, 65, 74; author's telephone interview with Castle, March 25, 2015.

2. Author's telephone interview with Castle, March 25, 2015; Labaco telephone interview with Castle, March 5, 2014.

3. Author's telephone interview with Castle, March 25, 2015.

4. Ibid.

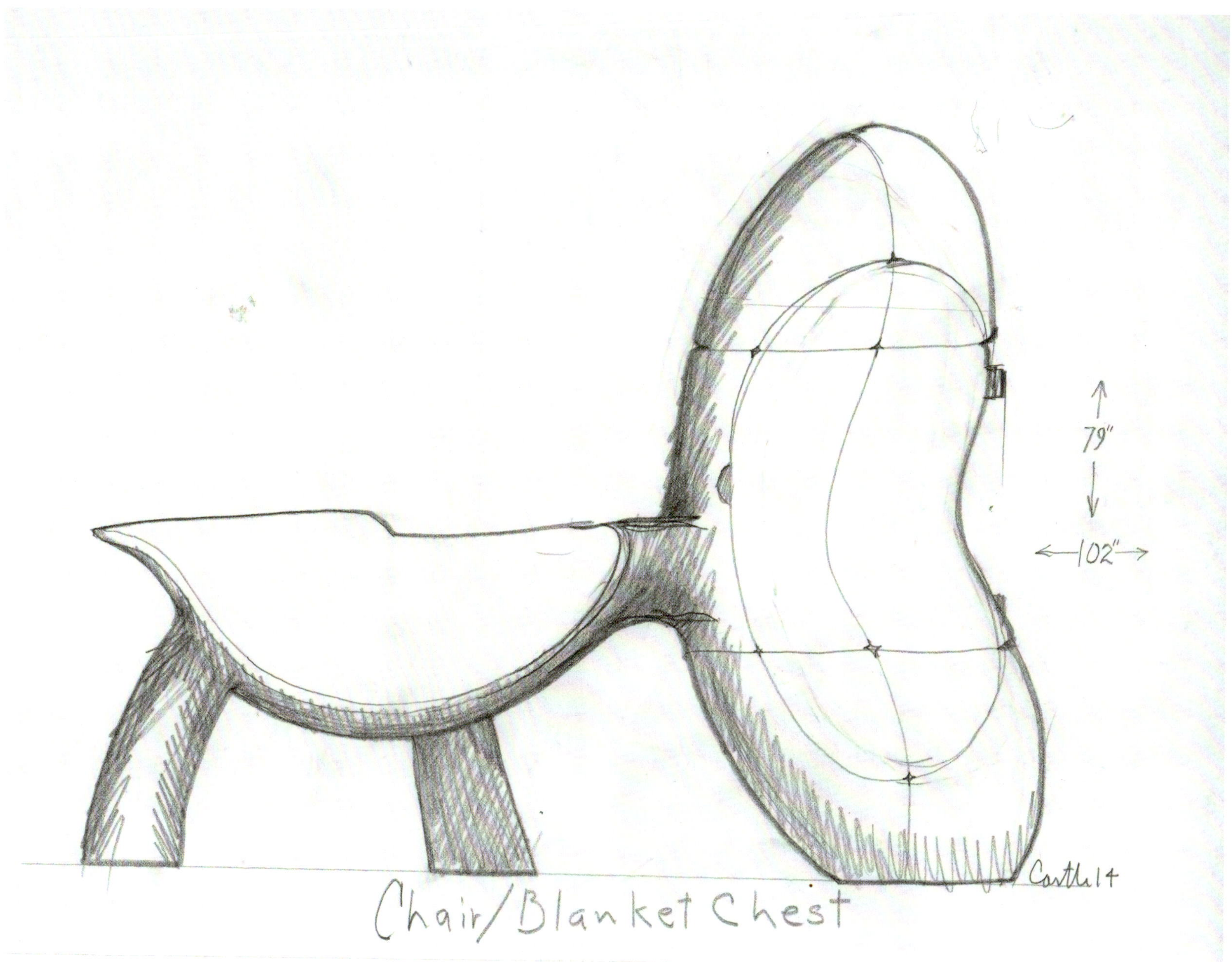

Plate 6

Remembering You, 2015

Designed with *Blanket Chest* (plate 4) in mind, *Remembering You* is an excellent example of Castle's reinvigoration of some of his most classic furniture forms. Here, he takes his combination furniture to a new level, integrating a cabinet, rather than adding a table (plate 7), to this chair—an unusual combination that makes one wonder at its purpose.

Regardless of its future function, it is clear that *Remembering You* reflects the methodology of Castle's current body of work, as well as that of earlier works. Its legs have a kinship to those of *Long Night* (plate 5), its peanut-shaped chest to the pomegranate form of *Blanket Chest*, and the biomorphic joinery between the two can be seen throughout Castle's current work—as if one of the chair's legs has suddenly transformed itself into the cabinet.

Chair with Table, 1964–1965

One of the most iconic elements of Castle's work is his use of combined forms. From the beginning of his career, he was interested in simplifying furniture pairings. If a table generally comes with a chair nearby, why not combine the two and reduce the number of legs involved? That was Castle's logic.[1] Combining pieces of furniture also creates more complex forms and allows for more sculptural possibilities, an important aspect in Castle's work.[2] This *Chair with Table* is the first instance of such a combined form.[3]

In this early iteration of combination furniture, the chair and table cantilever off of a central base—a very strong visual relationship is apparent between it and *Library Sculpture* (plates 9 and 10), which was made shortly after this piece. As a result of the uneven weight distribution between the chair and table portions, *Chair with Table* must be bolted to the floor as it cannot support itself.[4] At first, it seemed impossible to sell combined furniture forms. Many potential owners were hesitant to let the artist drill a hole in their living room floor in order to bolt the furniture down and commit fairly permanently to its placement.[5] As a result, Castle moved away from this model and began to experiment with balance.

Chair with Table was part of the Museum of Contemporary Crafts' 1966 exhibition, *Fantasy Furniture,* along with *Blanket Chest* (plate 4), *Library Sculpture,* and two additional works by Castle.[6]

1. Labaco telephone interview with Wendell Castle, August 7, 2014; author's telephone interview with Castle, February 9, 2015; Sims interview with Castle, March 24, 2015.

2. Labaco telephone interview with Wendell Castle, August 7, 2014.

3. Author's telephone interview with Castle, February 9, 2015; Eerdmans, *Wendell Castle: A Catalogue Raisonné,* 92.

4. Author's telephone interview with Castle, February 9, 2015; Gordon, *Wendell Castle: Wandering Forms,* 80.

5. Author's telephone interview with Castle, February 9, 2015.

6. *Fantasy Furniture* (New York: American Craftsmen's Council in association with the Museum of Contemporary Crafts, 1966), 12; Alastair Gordon, *Wendell Castle: Wandering Forms,* 87–88.

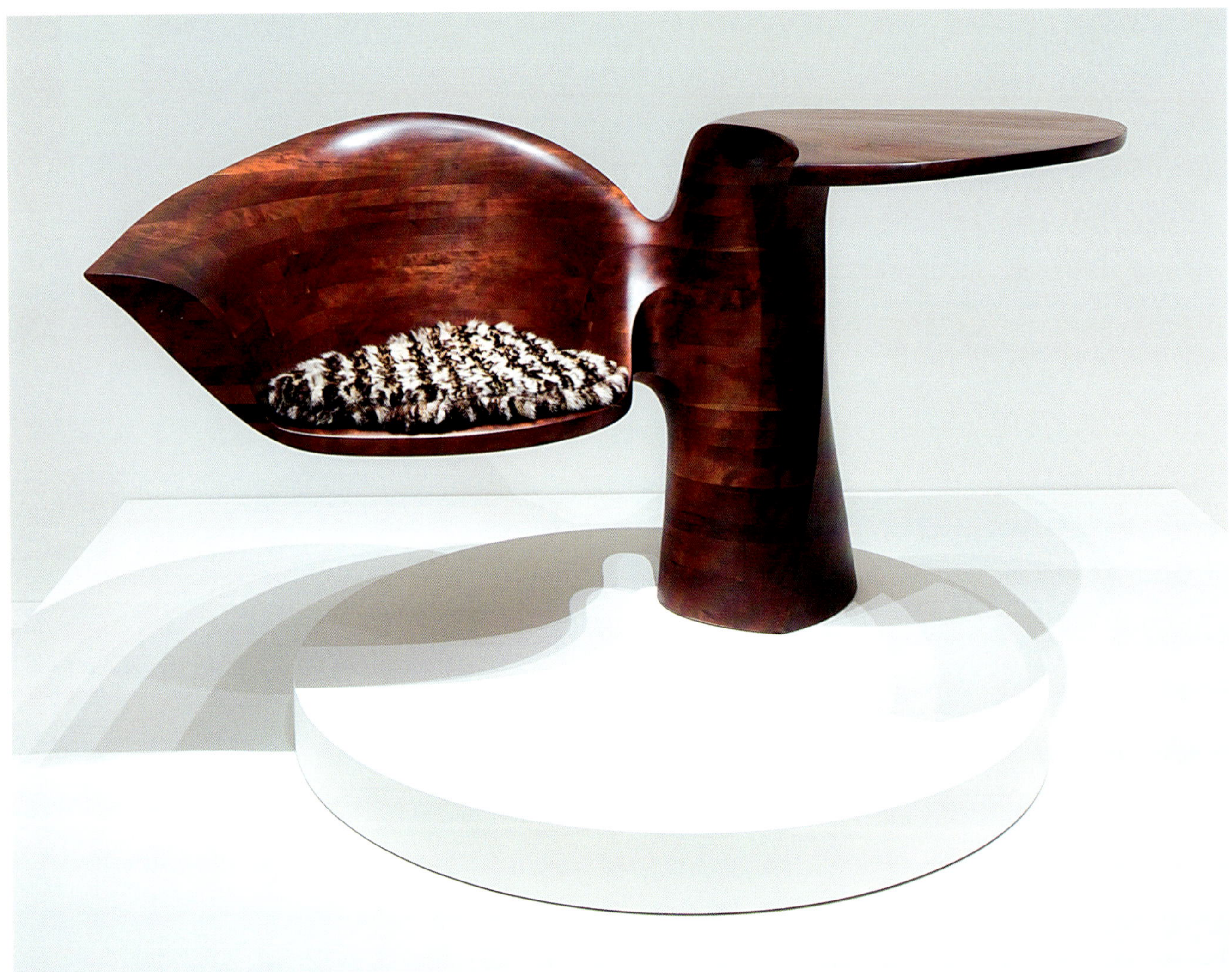

Plate 7

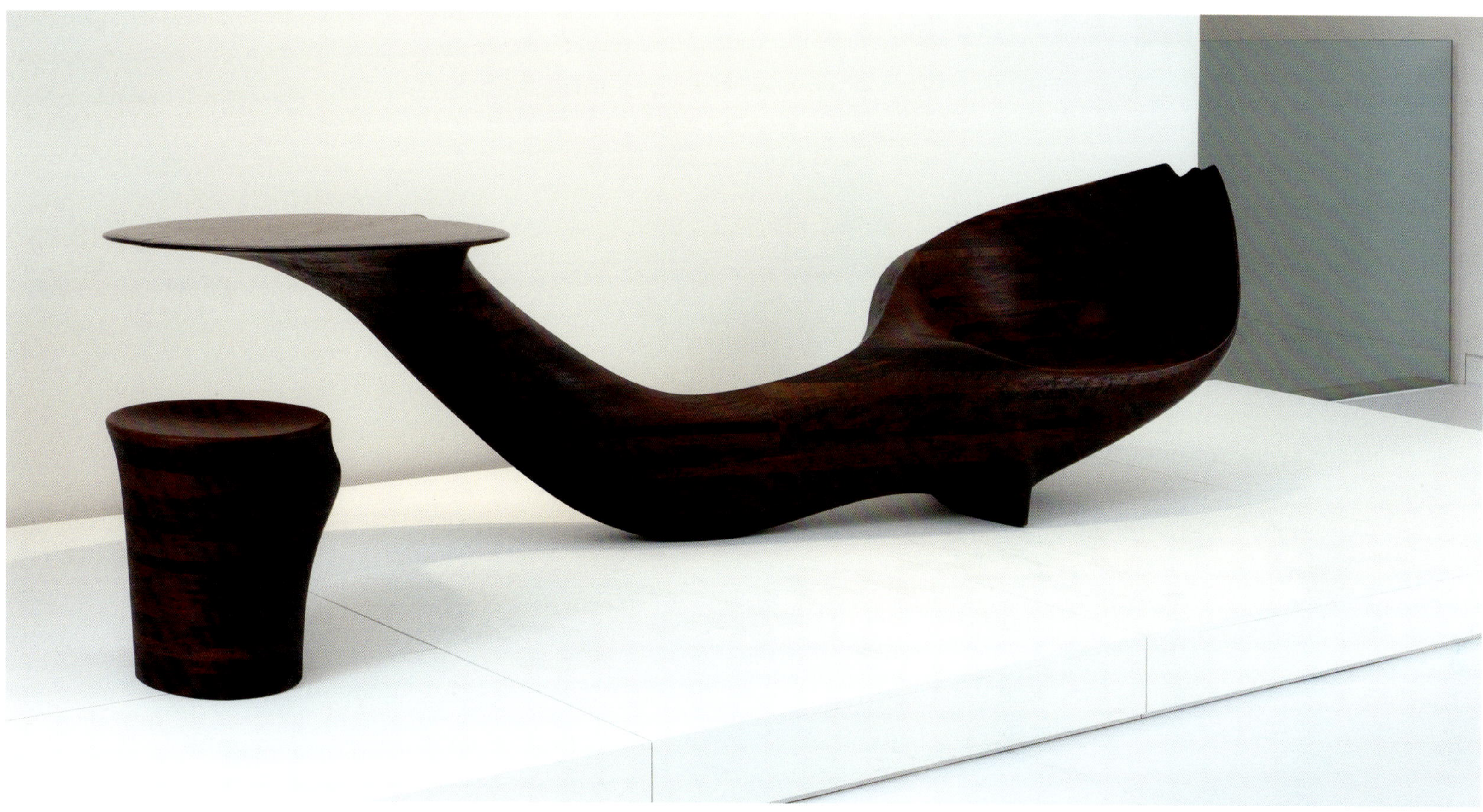

Plate 8

Table-Chair-Stool, 1968

As Castle's use of combined forms matured throughout the 1960s, he began to explore different vocabularies for expressing them. *Table-Chair-Stool* and the closely related *Chair with Table* (1968, plate 7) were the only pieces Castle made in this elongated, stretched-out vocabulary—something of a sea monster lurking just below the surface, with its long neck and flat head attached to a humped body.[1] Castle made these works for his first New York City exhibition at the Lee Nordness Gallery, *Handcrafted Furniture by Wendell Castle—New York Debut,* which took place in April 1968 and was what Nordness deemed to be the first solo exhibition given to an American artist/craftsman at a fine art gallery.[2] Nordness had long been impressed with Castle's work and was interested in asking him to join his gallery, but because he had showed solely paintings and sculptures thus far he wasn't sure what the reaction of the other artists would be; however, after seeing Castle's work in *Young Americans* and *Fantasy Furniture* at the Museum of Contemporary Crafts, Nordness became too enthusiastic not to show Castle's work.[3]

Chair with Table was purchased for the lobby of the Pacific Design Center in San Francisco and, when the building was sold, the chair/table went with it. The new owners kept the piece in their garden and as a result *Chair with Table* deteriorated over time. Due to the severity of the damage, it was eventually destroyed. *Table-Chair-Stool,* which is in the permanent collection of the Museum of Arts and Design, is now the only existing piece from this original pair.[4] In 2006, Castle revisited this form and created *Phoenix.*

1. Author's telephone interview with Castle, February 9, 2015.

2. Ibid.; Eerdmans, *Wendell Castle: A Catalogue Raisonné,* 98; Taragin et al., *Furniture by Wendell Castle,* 36.

3. Taragin et al., *Furniture by Wendell Castle,* 35–36.

4. Author's telephone interview with Castle, February 9, 2015.

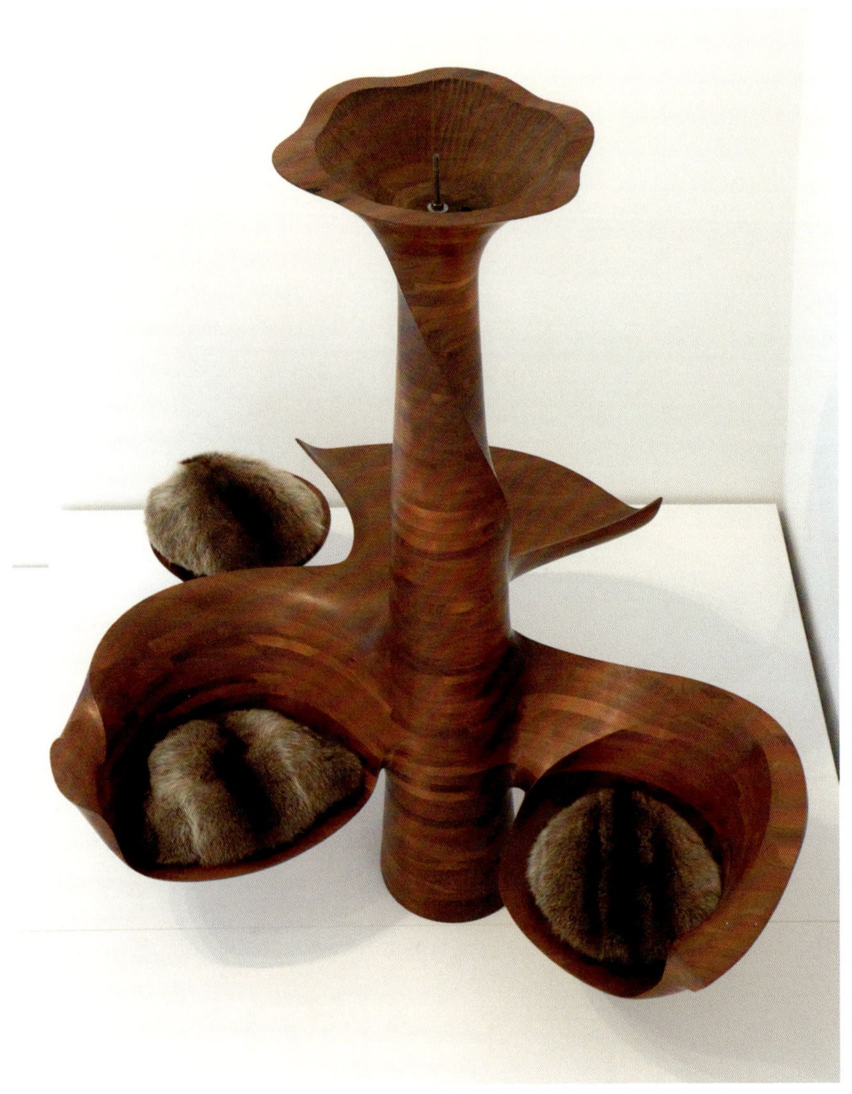

Plate 9

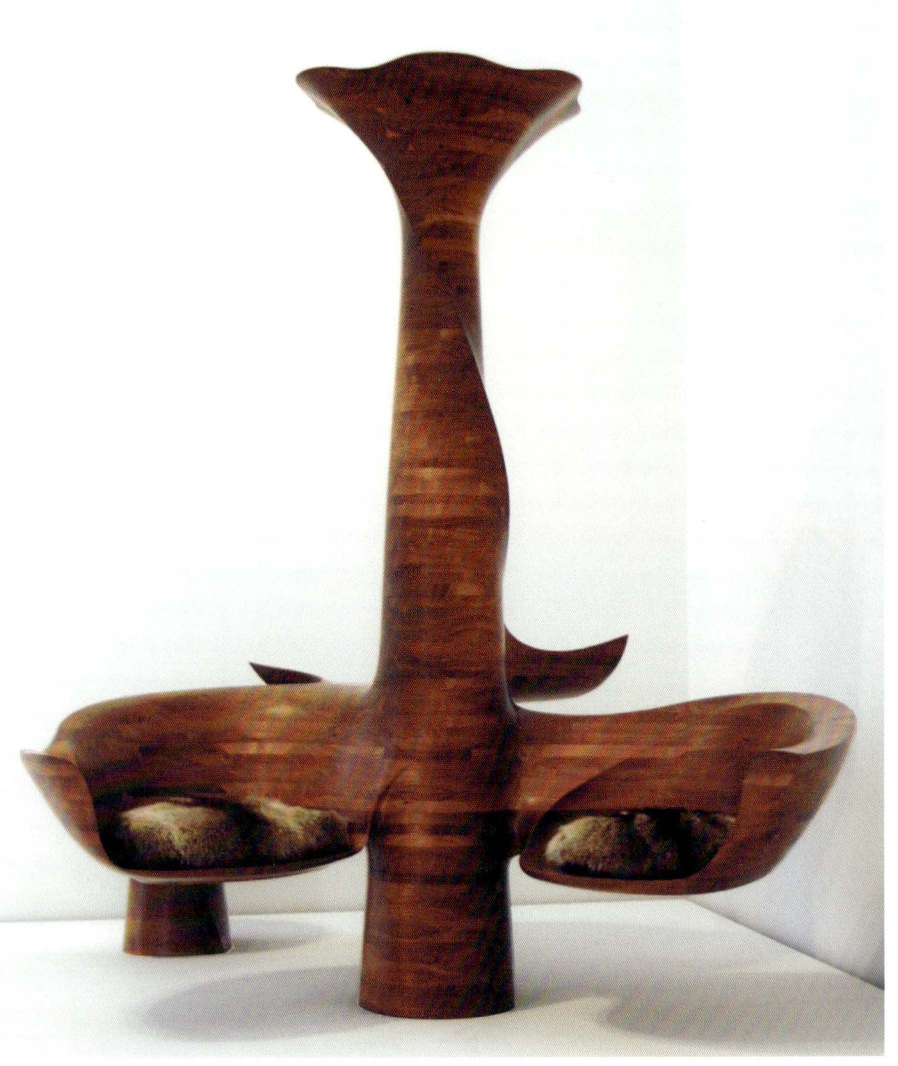

Plate 10

Serpentine Floor Lamp, 1965–1967

Lyrical in its elegance and evocative of the serpent from which it eventually took its name, it was actually the product of Castle playing with a paperclip until it reached an approximation of the shape seen in the piece.[1] He realized that this whiplash curve was fairly stable and began to incorporate it into his designs, resulting in this lamp and the closely related *Silver Leaf Desk* (1967).[2] Ever the lover of the large scale, Castle expanded on his use of height in *Library Sculpture* (plates 9 and 10) by an entire foot to create the monumental *Serpentine Floor Lamp*.[3]

In 1967, Paul J. Smith, former director of the Museum of Contemporary Crafts, curated *Acquisitions*, an exhibition that was organized in celebration of the tenth anniversary of the museum, and to "formally inaugurate the newest undertaking, an expanded acquisitions program designed to establish a permanent collection that will eventually be a thorough and systematic documentation of outstanding achievements in twentieth-century American crafts."[4] One-hundred-ninety artworks in wood, fiber, glass, ceramic, and metal were chosen for the exhibition, more than two-thirds of which were objects from the museum's permanent collection, with the remainder being objects identified by Smith as desired collection artworks.[5] Castle was represented by *Music Rack* (1964), which had entered the collection three years prior, and the exhibition marked the inaugural showing of his newly completed *Serpentine Floor Lamp*.[6]

1. Author's telephone interview with Castle, February 9, 2015.

2. Ibid.

3. Historically, this lamp has been dated to 1965, the date inscribed on its base. However, significant research has shown that the piece was completed in 1967 and the dating here reflects the full date range during which Castle created the lamp. Castle has confirmed that he did, in fact, use the date at which production or design began to date his work in the past, which accounts for the inscription of 1965 on its base. That, combined with the new research, supports this new dating of 1965–1967; author's telephone interview with Castle, March 25, 2015.

4. *Acquisitions* (New York: American Craftsmen's Council in association with the Museum of Contemporary Crafts, 1967), 1.

5. Ibid.

6. Ibid., 3; Museum of Contemporary Craft staff memo from Thomas Kyle to Paul J. Smith, April 24, 1967, Wendell Castle artist file, Museum of Arts and Design; letter from Wendell Castle to Thomas Kyle, May 11, 1967, Wendell Castle artist file, Museum of Arts and Design; two installation photographs of *Acquisitions* at the Museum of Contemporary Crafts, 1967, *Acquisitions* exhibition file, American Craft Council Library, Minneapolis, MN.

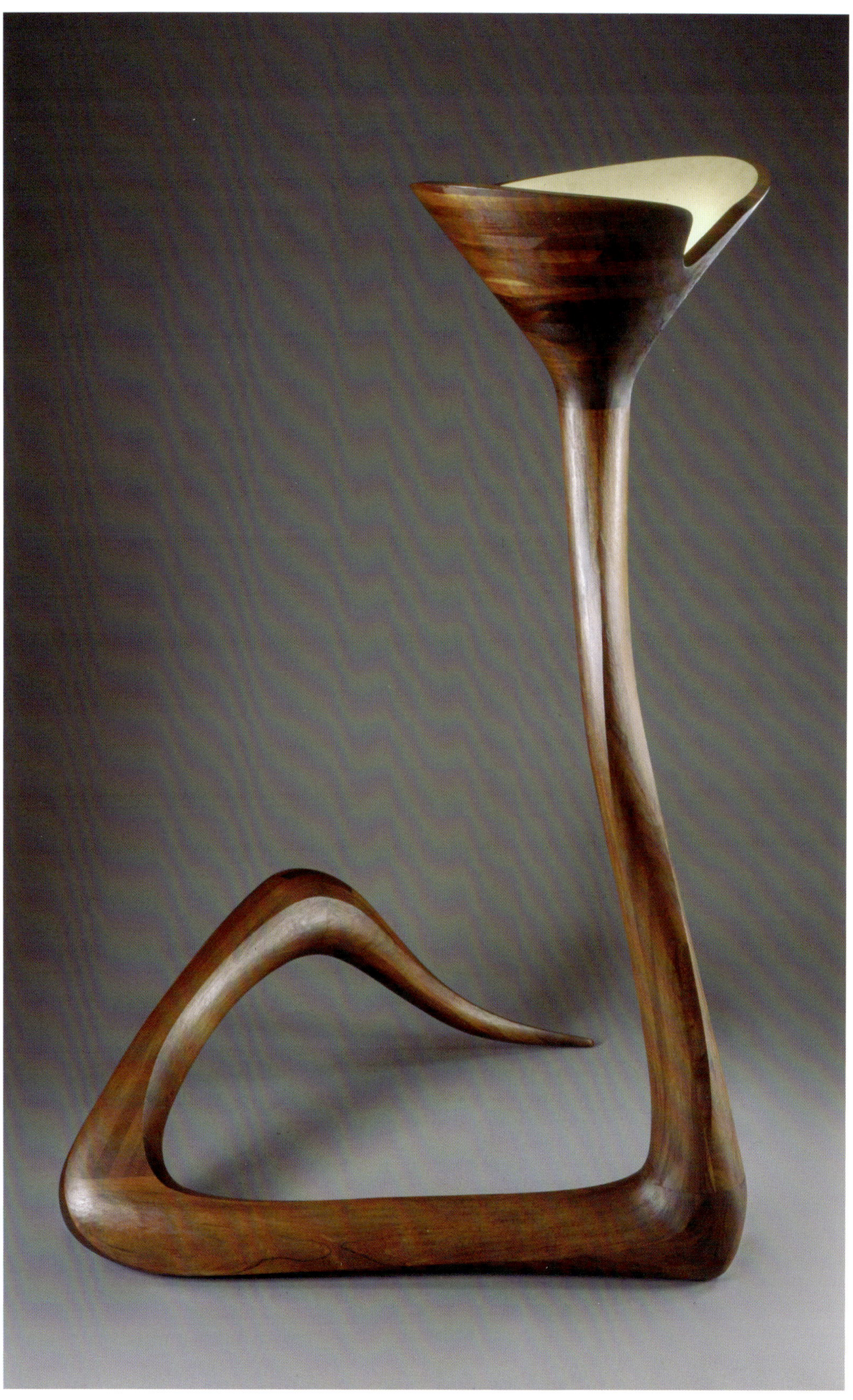

Plate 11

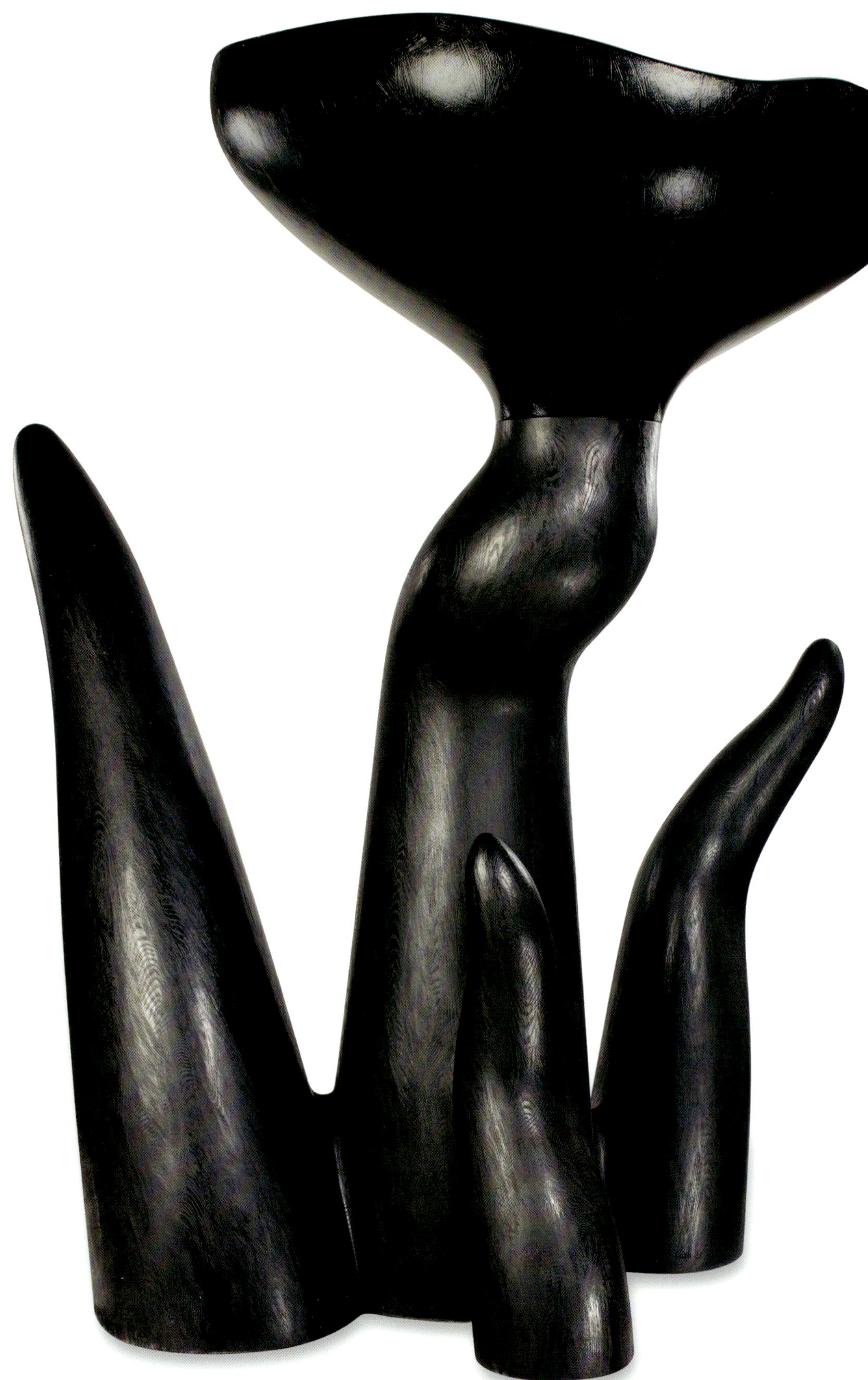

High Hopes, 2015

One of the most impressive pieces in Castle's newest body of work is *High Hopes*. At roughly nine feet tall, this lamp—its organic form that of a towering tree or mushroom—gives viewers the distinct feeling that they have tumbled down the rabbit hole into Wonderland and are awaiting an audience with the knowledgeable Caterpillar. Its lighting elements can be programmed to project multiple colors, shifting in a pattern that further emphasizes its fantastical qualities.

Castle's new shop motto—"go big or go home"—is evident after reviewing the breadth of his new work.[1] His love of scale pushed his works to become taller and more voluminous throughout the course of the 1960s, but now, with the help of the CNC machine, he can reach new heights. *High Hopes* is the epitome of what the Robot can do. Impossible without it, the long-reaching and flexible nature of the Robot's arm allows Castle to hollow out complex forms—not possible with the human hand purely because of restrictions in reach and movement.[2] This, in turn, allows Castle's work to reach monumental sizes without becoming exponentially heavier.

1. Author's telephone interview with Castle, March 25, 2015.
2. Cheatle and Jackson, "Digital Entanglements: Craft, Computation and Collaboration in Fine Arts Furniture Production," 9.

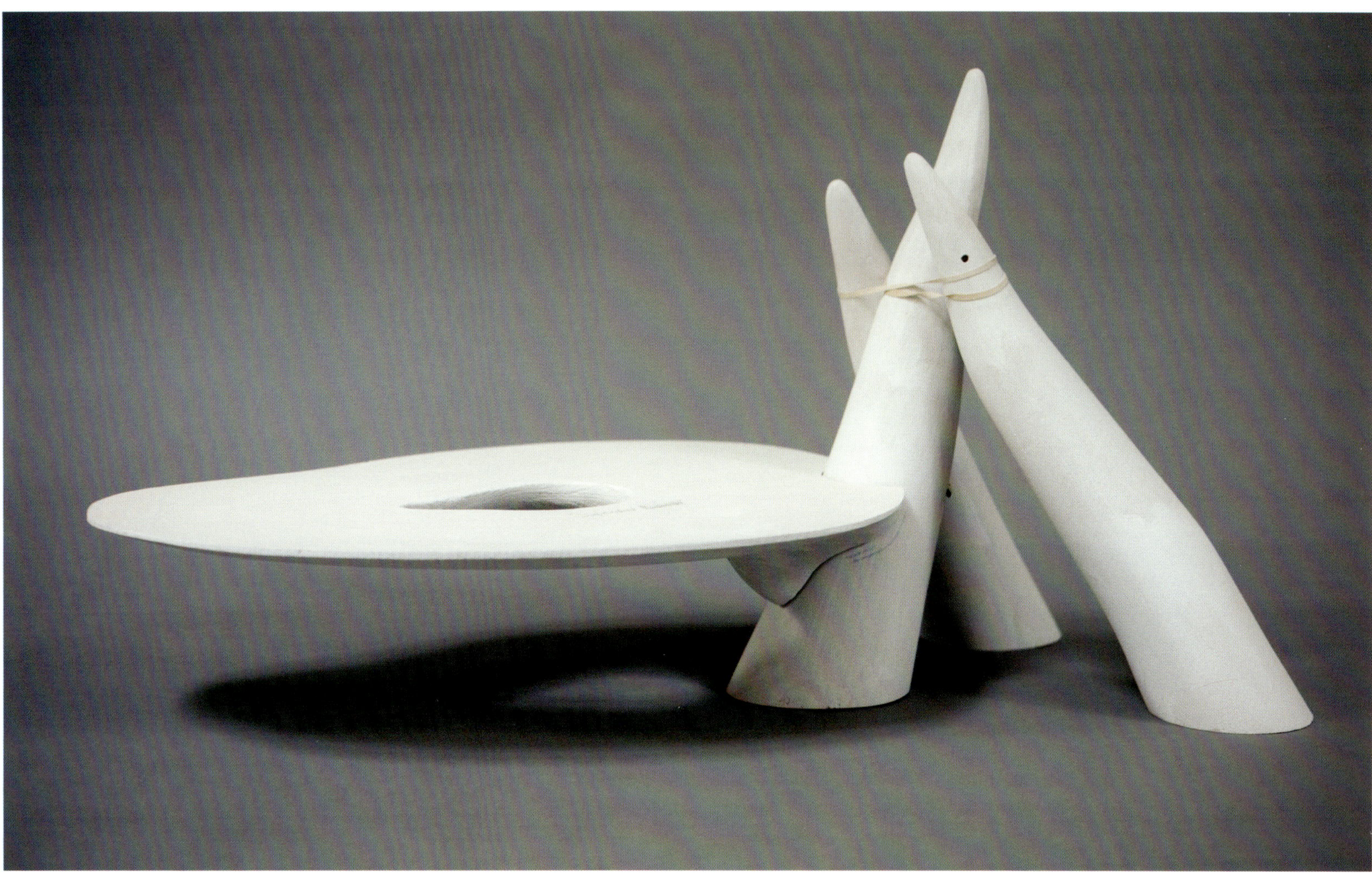

Suspended Disbelief, 2015

Castle's 2015 *Suspended Disbelief* is directly influenced by his *Dining Table* of 1966 (plate 14). While he didn't want to try to outdo his successful and elegant earlier design, he was able to update it to reflect his new vocabulary of forms and technological capabilities.

An organic tabletop with a central hole closely resembles the earlier table, but as a point of difference it dramatically cantilevers—thanks to the ability of the CNC machine, the Robot, to create areas of joinery with exacting precision—away from a sculptural element, to the side. This sculptural element is comprised of three overlapping cones, the tallest point reaching nearly seven feet, which represents the visual language of Castle's most recent work.

Dining Table, 1966

When looking through the breadth of Castle's work over the course of nearly six decades, it is clear that he favors chairs. Although he had made a few smaller tables, up until this point he had avoided making large tables and dining tables. Because Castle creates his furniture with the hand of a sculptor, the most interesting part of the table for him to create is the base.[1] The base allows for much more freedom of form than does a tabletop, which needs to be level and flat.[2] The larger the table, the more the top will hide the base and any potential for sculptural elements.[3] With this *Dining Table*, Castle's first, he solved this problem by ingeniously cutting a hole directly in the center of the tabletop, which opens up the line of vision to the base below, allowing for another sightline to the table's more sculptural qualities.[4]

Dining Table currently resides in Castle's own home, where he and his wife use it daily. Originally made for his own use, Castle sold it to a friend—after much insistence—about a year after it was produced. In the 1990s, the table entered the market, Castle purchased it back, and it now has a permanent place in his own collection.[5]

Dining Table is one of three closely related tables: a larger dining table that Castle made for Drs. Paul and Gloria Choi, and a coffee table that he made for gallery owner Lee Nordness—the first iteration of this form—complete the series.[6]

1. Author's telephone interview with Castle, February 9, 2015; Taragin et al., *Furniture by Wendell Castle*, 30.

2. Author's telephone interview with Castle, February 9, 2015.

3. Ibid.

4. Ibid.

5. Ibid.

6. Ibid.; Gordon, *Wandering Forms*, 80.

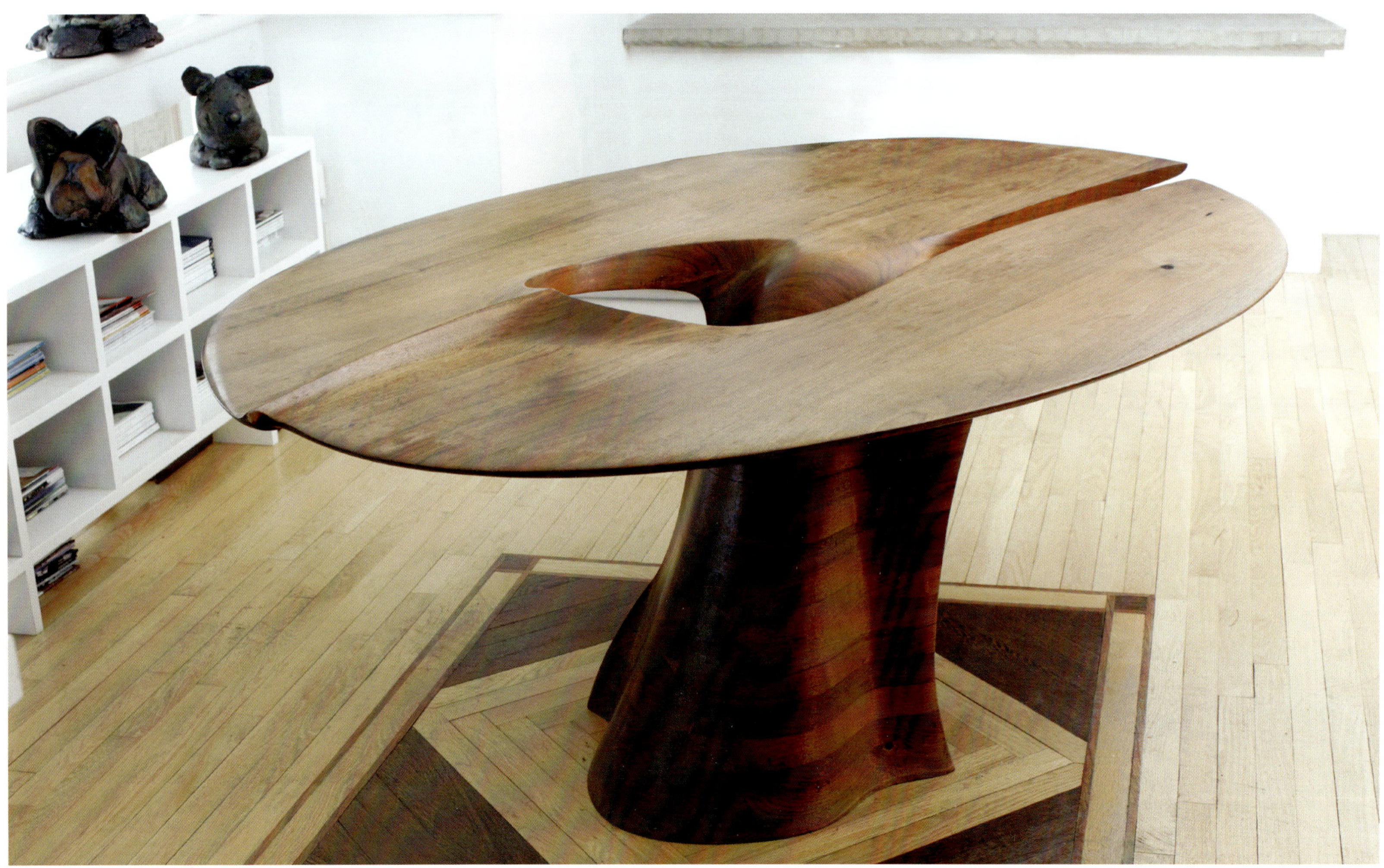

Plate 14

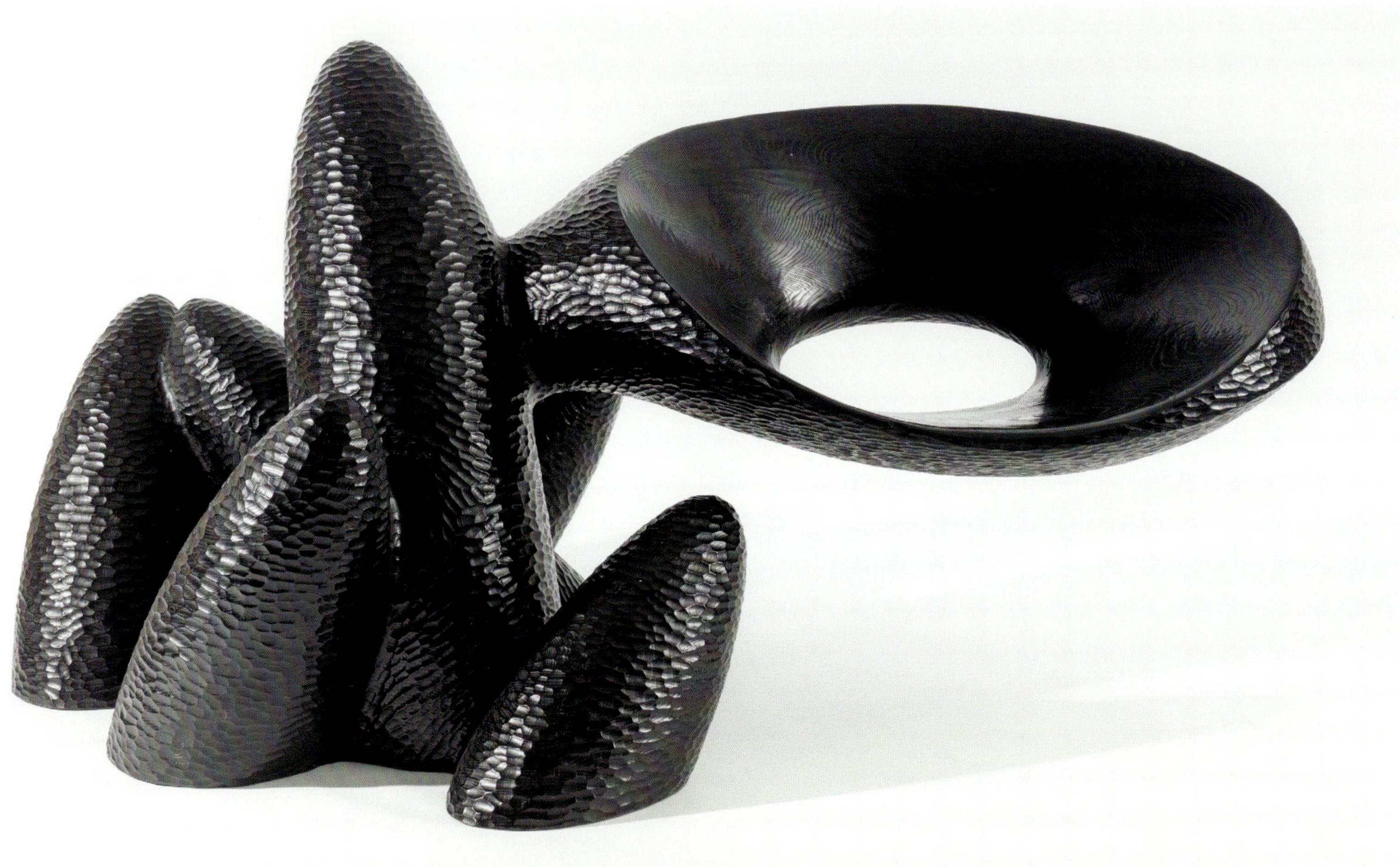

Plate 15

1. Labaco telephone interview with Castle, March 5, 2014.

2. Ron Labaco telephone interview with Marvin Pallischeck, August 1, 2014.

3. Author's telephone interview with Castle, March 25, 2015.

4. Ron Labaco and author's interview with Wendell Castle, Scottsville, NY, February 24, 2015; Sims interview with Castle, Scottsville, NY, March 24, 2015.

Wind Songs, 2015

Castle's design process focuses around drawing.[1] He's never far from his sketch pad and his drawings seem to cover the studio like handcrafted bits of confetti.[2] As he "works out" his designs on paper—he never works with the computer during this stage—he references a vocabulary of forms that he has mentally tucked away over the years.[3] There are some elements that creep up again and again, sometimes within a certain body of work and sometimes at different points in his career.

In this most recent body of work, Castle explores the use of tendril forms, which seem to evolve through a life cycle, from the seedlings or buds of *Wind Songs* through the growth stage illustrated in *Never Ask*, maturing into the strong cones of *Wandering Mountain* (plate 27). Castle uses these elements to create compositions or clusters.[4] Elements of these forms can also be seen in *Above-Within-Beyond* (plate 16), *More or Less* (plate 29), and *High Hopes* (plate 12).

Above-Within-Beyond, 2014

The University of Kansas, where Castle received his MFA in sculpture, was one of the first universities in the United States to have a professional foundry for metal casting.[1] As a result, it became a major part of the school's curriculum and Castle did a significant amount of bronze casting during his time there.[2] In fact, he put himself through school by making commissioned portrait busts.[3] After graduation, he couldn't afford to continue his work at a professional foundry, so he stopped working in bronze.[4] In the 1990s, while he was represented by the Peter Joseph Gallery in New York City, he experimented again with metal casting and created *Angel Chair,* in patinated bronze.[5] In 2008, while with Friedman Benda—his current gallery representation—Castle created *Abilene Rocking Chair* in cast stainless steel.[6]

Above-Within-Beyond is one of the first in Castle's new series of cast-bronze works. Its mammoth size takes the piece beyond—as its name suggests—interior use to the world of outdoor sculpture, along with *Wandering Mountain* (plate 27) and *Temptation* (plate 26). Although they are still functional, because of their increasing size and use outdoors, these pieces push the boundaries of Castle's furniture even farther into the sculptural realm than his stack-laminated chairs do.

1. Oral history interview with Wendell Castle, June 3–December 12, 1981, Archives of American Art; author's telephone interview with Castle, March 25, 2015.

2. Author's telephone interview with Castle, March 25, 2015.

3. Ibid.

4. Ibid.

5. Ibid.; Eerdmans, *Wendell Castle: A Catalogue Raisonné,* 322–323.

6. Author's telephone interview with Castle, March 25, 2015; *Wendell Castle: Unflinching Faith,* Friedman Benda, http://www.friedmanbenda.com/exhibitions/wendell-castle-unflinching-faith, accessed March 28, 2015; Eerdmans, *Wendell Castle: A Catalogue Raisonné,* 397.

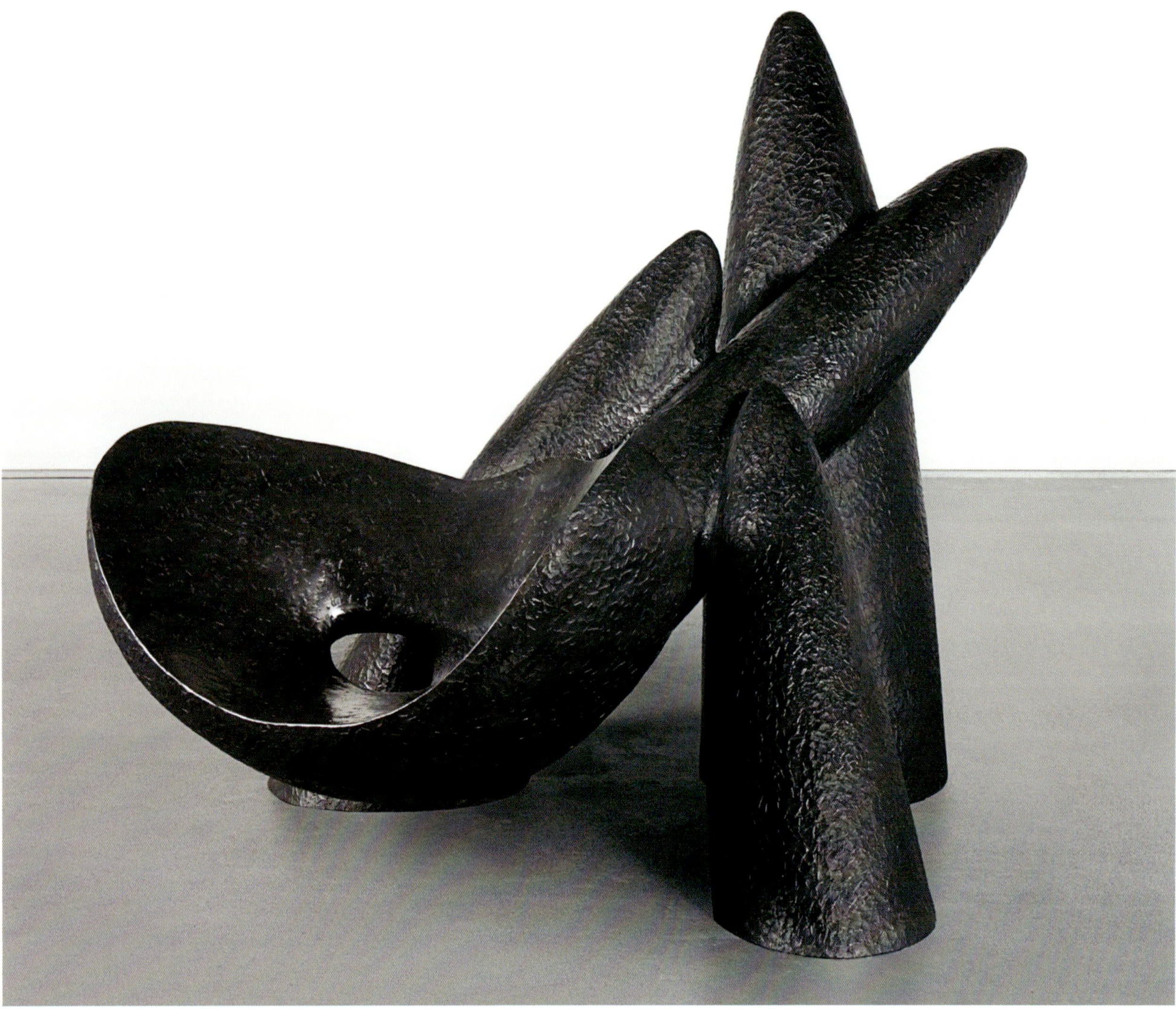

Plate 16

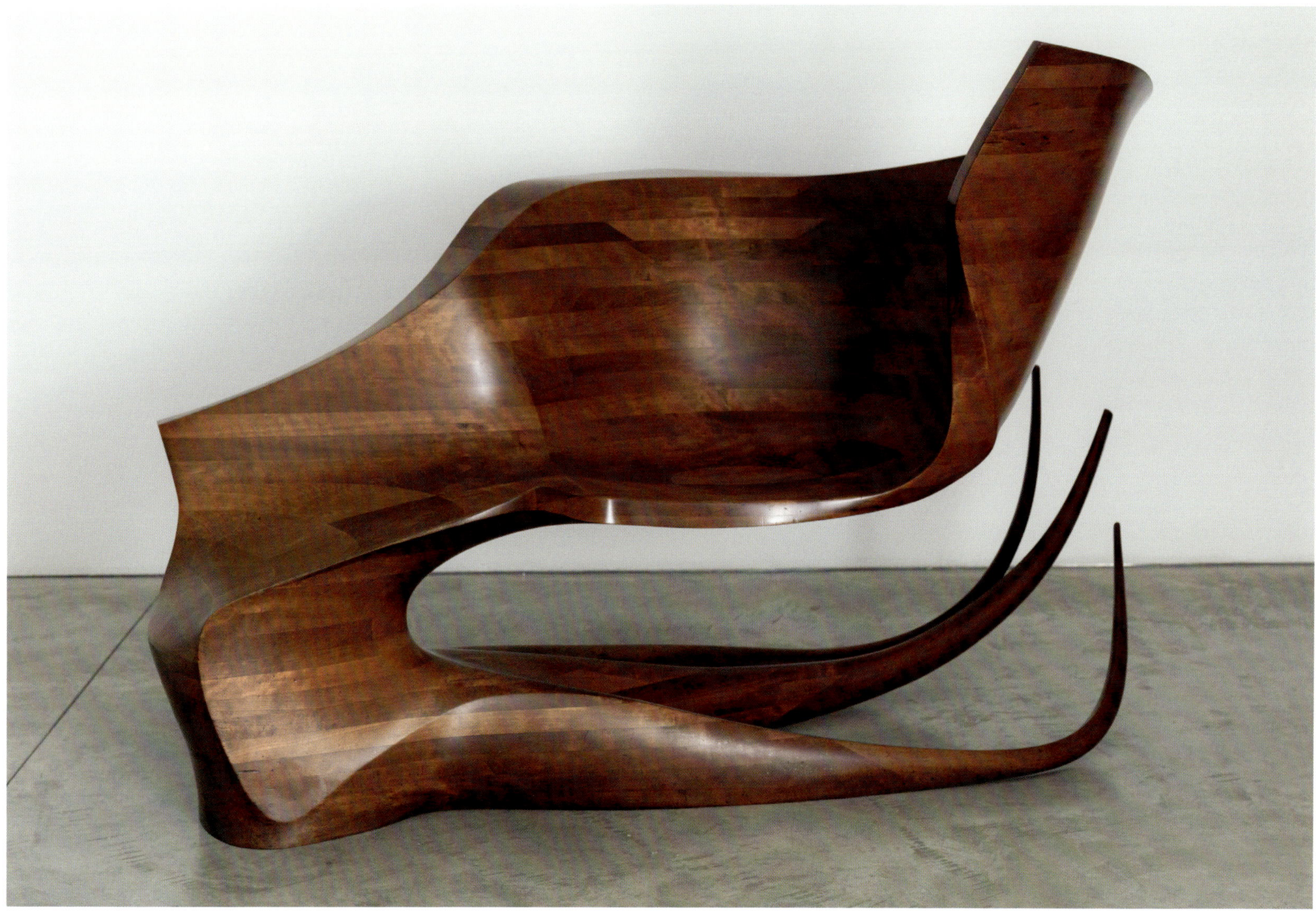

Squid Chair No. 1, 1966

Prior to the late 1970s, Castle did not give his work formal titles; however, after twenty years of making chairs, tables, and chair/tables, it became difficult to verbally distinguish between works without describing them. Starting with explanations of type, such as "chair" or "table," the descriptions began to morph into names, and it is easy to see how this chair with its tentacle-like protrusions became known as *Squid Chair.*[1] After the 1970s, Castle began giving his forms more abstract titles in the manner of fine art, which emphasized his ability to transcend the furniture world into that of sculpture.

These tentacles—related to those of *Stool* (plate 3)—also play a practical purpose and mark a relationship between *Squid Chair No. 1* and *Chair with Table* (plate 7).[2] To solve the problem of having to bolt furniture to the floor, Castle realized he could continue to make combination furniture if he allowed himself to work with more weight.[3] Heavier works could be self-balancing and counterweights could be provided for cantilevered elements.[4] By committing himself to heavier works, he could create more dynamic and sculptural forms that played with the idea of balance or lack of balance, while still being stable pieces of furniture, as seen here.[5]

1. Author's telephone interview with Castle, February 9, 2015.
2. Ibid.
3. Ibid.; Gordon, *Wendell Castle: Wandering Forms,* 80.
4. Author's telephone interview with Castle, February 9, 2015.
5. Ibid.

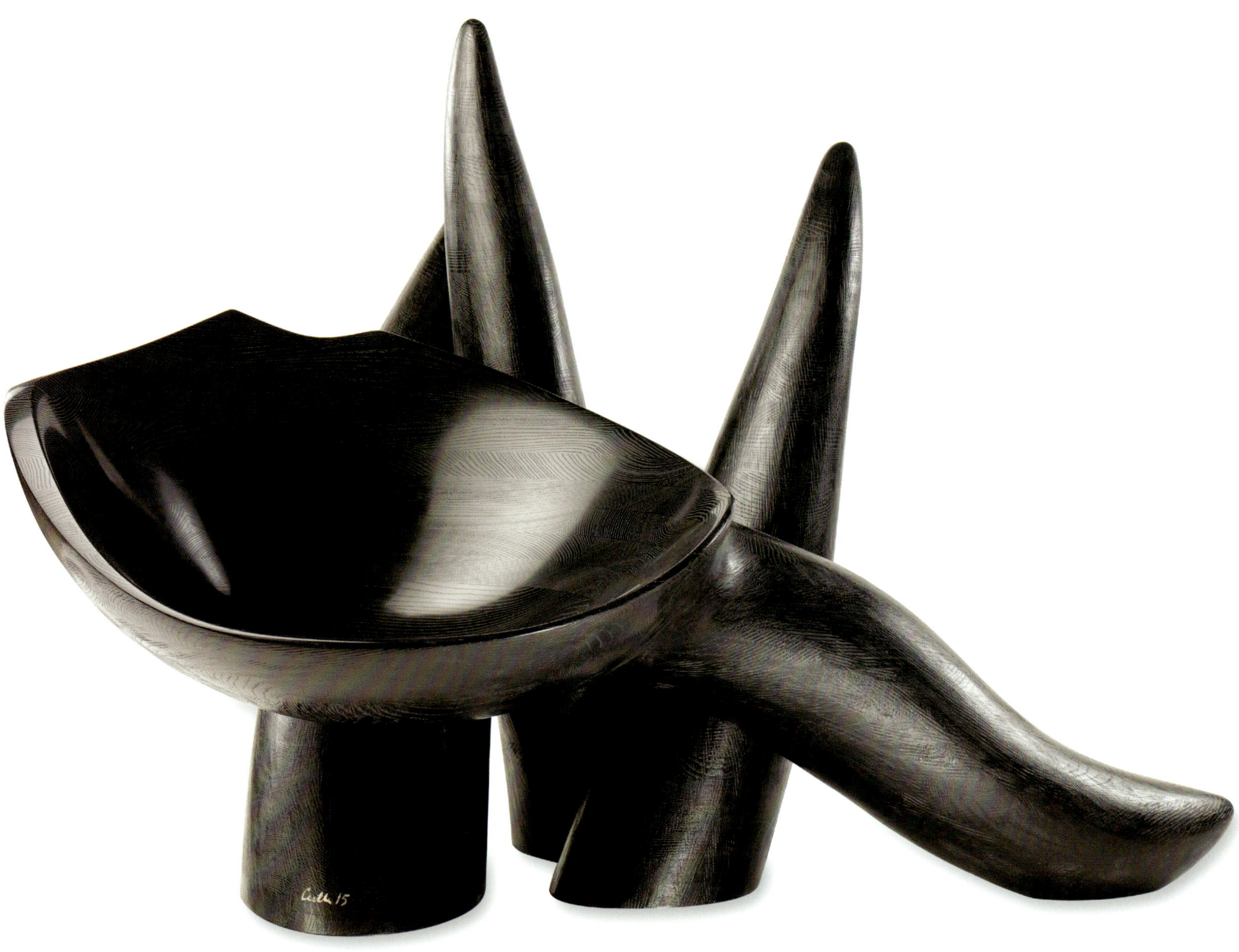

Plate 18

Never Ask, 2015

As Castle continued to design with these tendrils, they began to take on a more organic form, something that is never far from his work. In fact, Castle is always quick to attribute nature, particularly plant life, as one of his most prominent design influences.[1] As such, it's not surprising to see that although they are wider and more cylindrically shaped, these tendrils reflect the tentacle elements of *Stool* (plate 3) and *Squid Chair No. 1* (plate 17). In addition to a consistent interest in nature and the organic, this shows that Castle reincorporates details into his work that he feels are particularly strong.

1. Labaco and author's interview with Castle, Scottsville, NY, February 24, 2015.

52

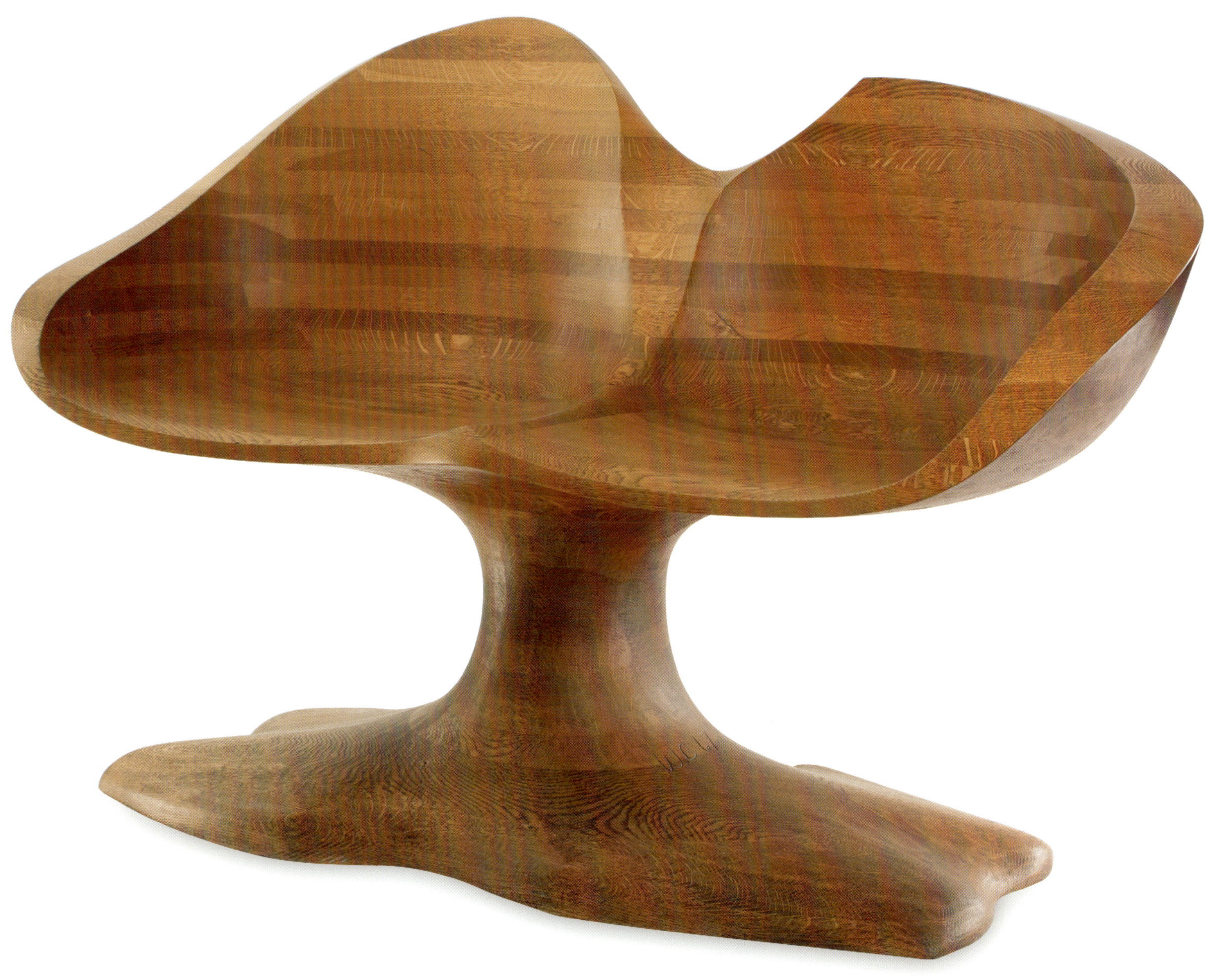

Plate 19

Double Chair, 1967

Another form that is an iconic part of Castle's oeuvre is the double chair. Sometimes called a settee, Castle's double-seated forms are perhaps more evocative of a love seat. In *Double Chair*, the individual seats, defined by two distinct chair backs and a barely visible central divide, have a sense of separateness; however, their ergonomic design and slightly slouching posture creates an intimate atmosphere. As with much of Castle's furniture, *Double Chair* plays with the relationships between its occupants, as well as those between its occupants and the furniture itself.

Castle himself has a special relationship to this particular two-seater, which is the very first in a long line of double chairs, preceded only by the *Baker Two-Seater*, which was a much more traditional settee form.[1] A breakthrough in form, *Double Chair* is part of Castle's personal collection, where it has been since it was created.[2]

1. Eerdmans, *Wendell Castle: A Catalogue Raisonné*, 95.

2. Author's telephone interview with Castle, February 9, 2015.

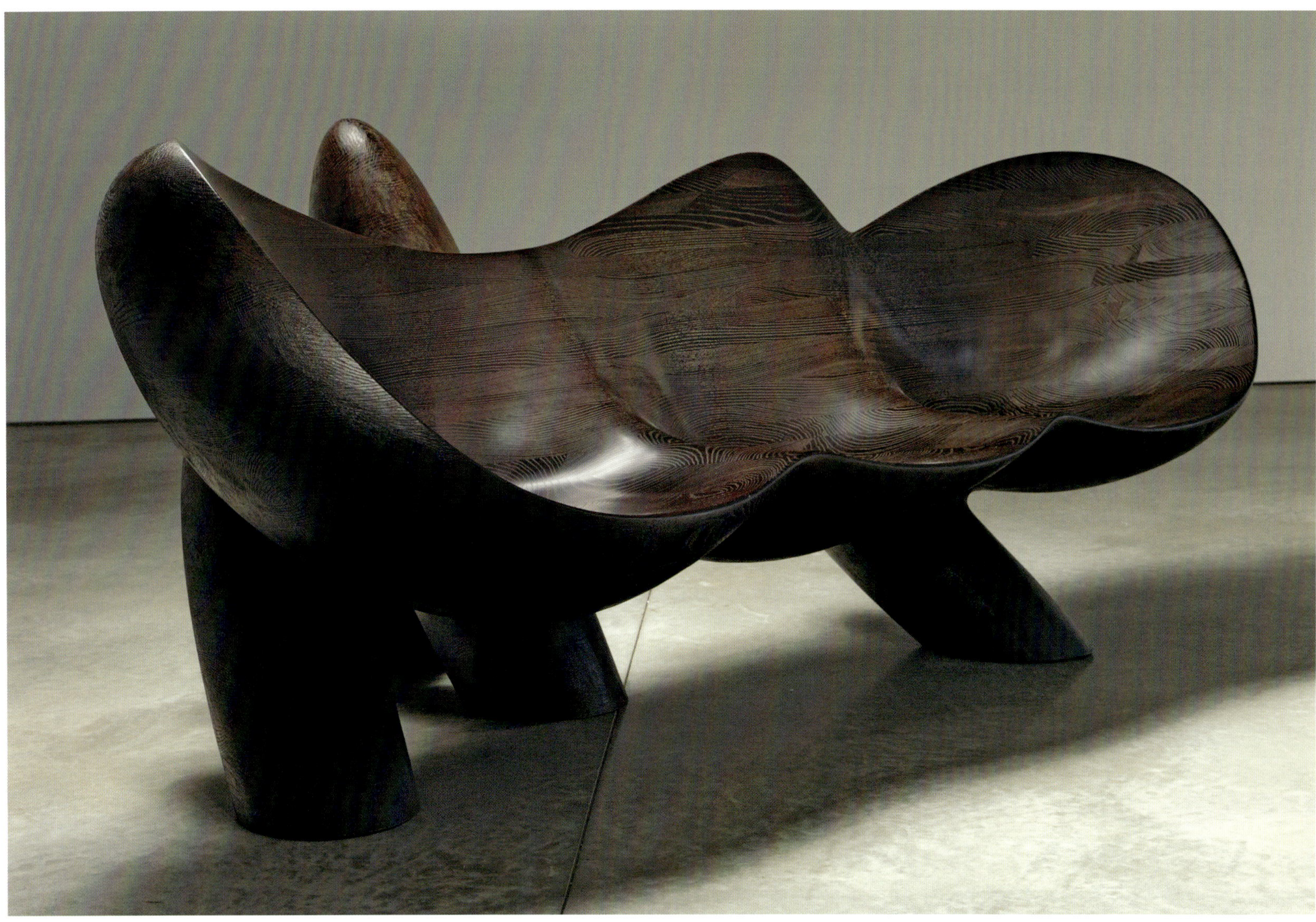

Plate 20

The Secret of a Few, 2012

In addition to making multiples in wood easier, Castle's adoption of digital technology assists him in creating larger-scale works. He did make large works in the 1960s, including *Library Sculpture* (plates 9 and 10) and *Serpentine Floor Lamp* (plate 11), as well as site-specific commissions such as the *Baker Dining Table* (1966); *Great Sofa* (1967) for the apartment of Lee Nordness; *Bed*, which includes a desk, lamp, chest of drawers, and night table; and finally a three-seat *Settee* (1967) that is in the collection of The Art Institute of Chicago.[1] Even so, these were few and far between.

With the CNC milling machine, the large-scale works are facilitated in a way that allows Castle to create many more. With the Robot making the initial rough cuts for many works, Castle is freed up to create additional pieces and his assistants can dedicate their work more readily to skilled tasks, increasing the overall output of the studio.[2] The use of this tool allows Castle to achieve more sophistication in form in a relatively short amount of time.

1. Eerdmans, *Wendell Castle: A Catalogue Raisonné,* 107, 136–137.

2. Labaco telephone interview with Pallischeck, August 1, 2014; Cheatle and Jackson, "Digital Entanglements: Craft, Computation and Collaboration in Fine Arts Furniture Production," 8.

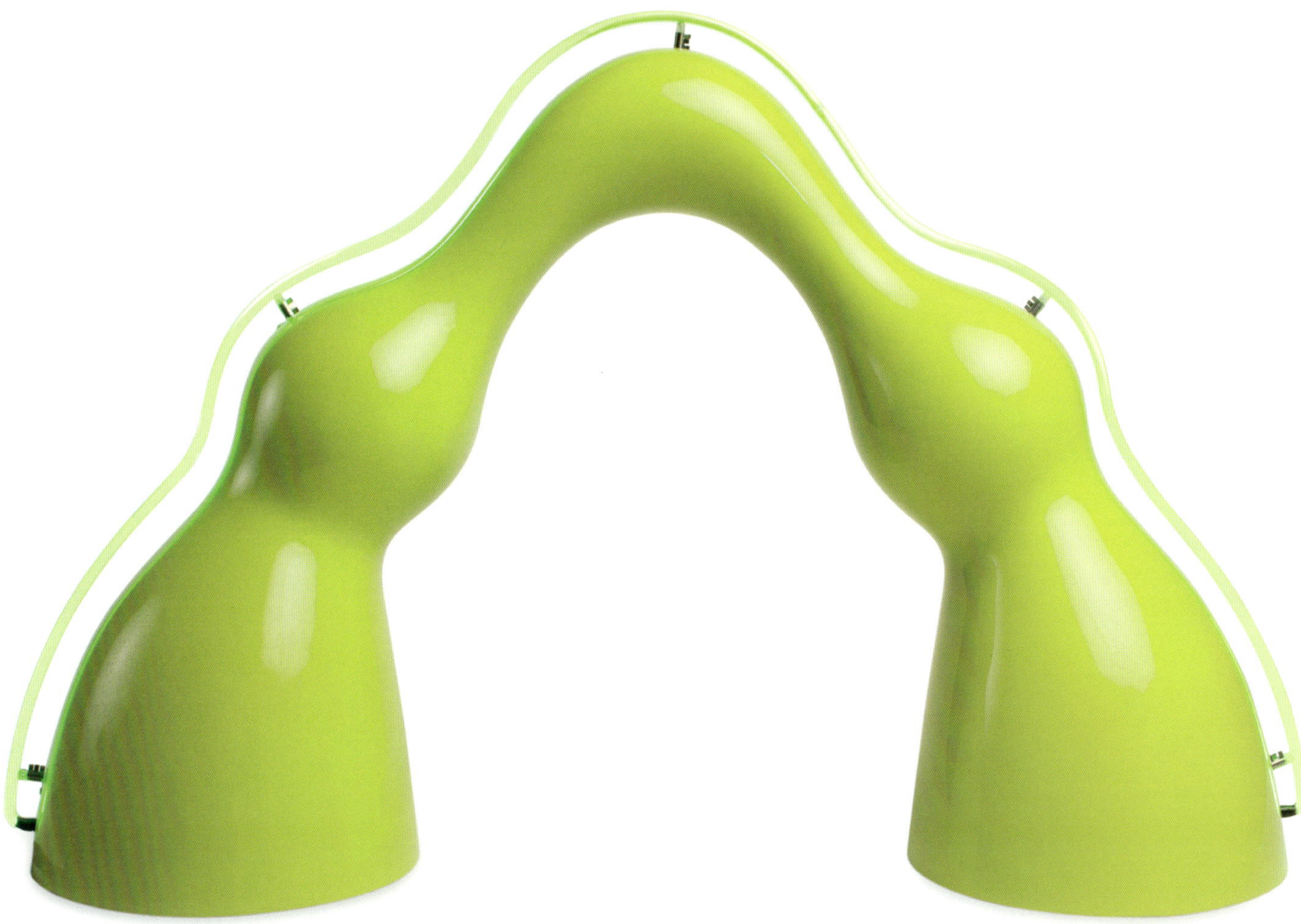

Plate 21

Benny, 1969

In 1970, Lee Nordness Gallery held the exhibition *Sculpted Furniture Forms*; originally meant to be a show that included multiple furniture forms—as the title suggests—it developed into an exhibition of lamps.[1] Castle designed eight new fiberglass lamps, including *Benny*, one of the earliest, for the show.[2] These early lamps were cast from the same arch-shaped mold and were differentiated by their individually colored gel-coat finishes—a type of resin that hardens to a shiny finish—and lighting elements.[3] Within the same year, Castle evolved beyond the initial mold and began to create new lamp forms from cut-up and reassembled mold pieces, expanding on his initial design.[4]

Out of all of the lamps, *Benny* is particularly notable as it is Castle's first use of neon, a popular material in contemporary sculpture at the time, which again asserts Castle's place as an artist whose work straddles both the craft and fine art worlds.[5] The lamps' existence as sculpture is further seen in their forms. They are sculptural first and lamps second, and in many cases—such as *Benny*, which includes only neon—barely a lamp at all. Such a methodology is fitting and in keeping with Castle's rejection of the frequently touted "form follows function." Lee Nordness said it best: "These are incidentally sculptures which happen to light."[6]

1. Gordon, *Wendell Castle: Wandering Forms*, 171; Eerdmans, *Wendell Castle: A Catalogue Raisonné,* 42.

2. Ibid.

3. Eerdmans, *Wendell Castle: A Catalogue Raisonné,* 42.

4. Ibid.

5. Taragin, et al., *Furniture by Wendell Castle,* 37.

6. Gordon, *Wendell Castle: Wandering Forms*, 171.

Castle Chair, 1969

Nowhere does Castle's sense of humor and lightheartedness come through more than in his gel-coated, fiberglass-reinforced plastic furniture. Inspired by George Sugarman's painted and laminated sculptures, and Italian postwar design, particularly the work of Joe Colombo and Ettore Sottsass, these Pop-art-esque colors and forms come straight out of the psychedelic '60s, and yet do not stray entirely from Castle's playful yet carefully handcrafted stack-laminated works.[1] It was Castle's quest for color that led him away from wood and toward plastics in 1968, when he began experimenting with painting over wood.[2] That less-than-satisfactory method of introducing color into his work paved the way for what would eventually become fiberglass furniture created through a molding process. Plastics provided Castle with a faster and freer means of working and allowed him to circumvent rising lumber costs.[3] The eponymous *Castle Chair* is an early example of his expansion into this medium.

1. Sims interview with Castle, Scottsville, NY, March 24, 2015; Taragin et al., *Furniture by Wendell Castle*, 36, 42.

2. Sims interview with Castle, Scottsville, NY, March 24, 2015; Gordon, *Wendell Castle: Wandering Forms*, 128; Taragin et al., *Furniture by Wendell Castle*, 36.

3. Gordon, *Wendell Castle: Wandering Forms*, 130.

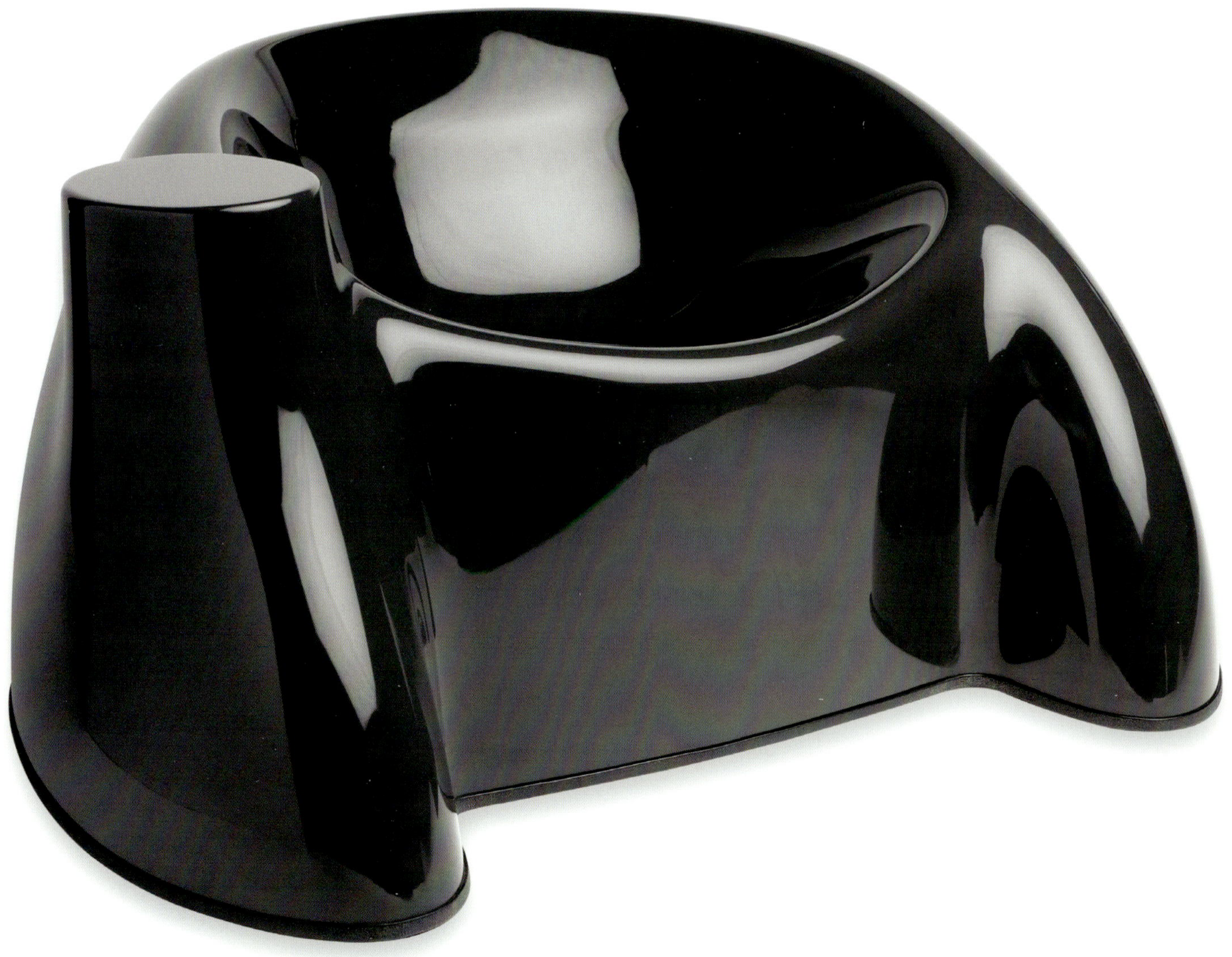

Plate 22

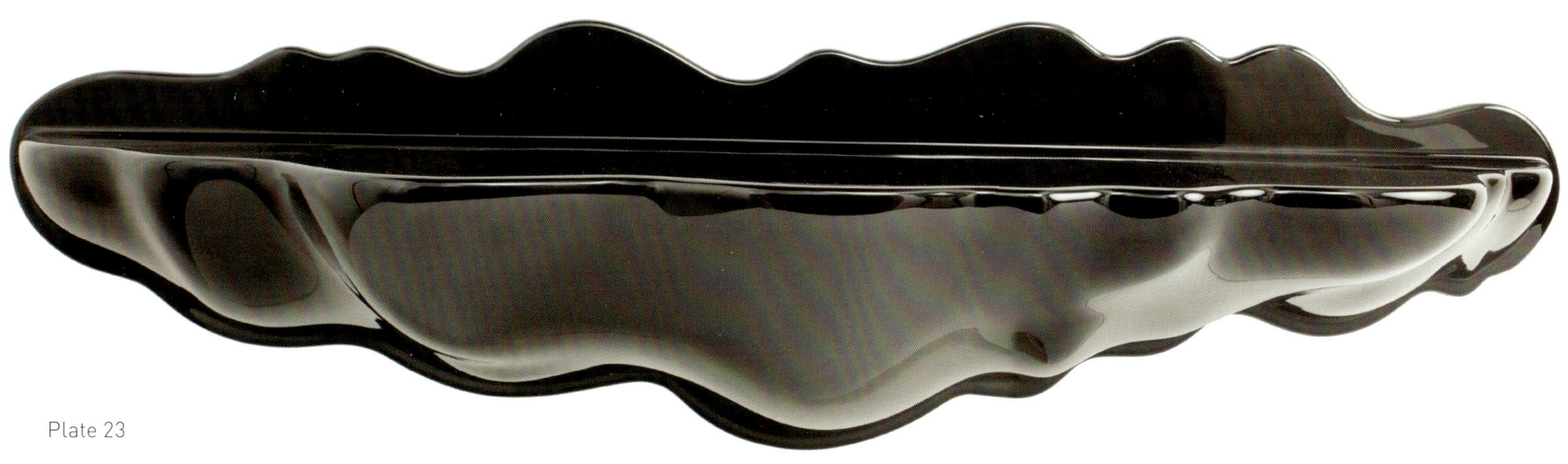

Plate 23

Cloud Shelf, 1969

Soon after *Castle Chair* (plate 22), Castle expanded his plastic furniture into what would become known as the *Molar Group*. It included an armchair, side chair, settee, two dining and coffee tables, a child's chair and lamp, and *Cloud Shelf*.[1] Whimsical in white, the black *Cloud Shelf* takes on a more ominous tone. Its high-gloss finish, evocative of thickly coated oil, accentuates its voluminous form.

Gel-coated, fiberglass-reinforced plastic was the perfect medium for Castle to expand on his use of volume, a central theme of his furniture. The fiberglass works were made through a molding process and Castle made the plugs from which these molds were created—essentially building up what would become negative space. Their hollow insides, matched with the shiny, boldly colored exteriors, create a balloon effect, as if these pieces, *Cloud Shelf* included, have been inflated.

While Castle created all of the plugs—or forms—the actual fiberglass work was done in limited production at Northern Plastics in Syracuse, New York.[2] The ability to make multiples from one plug allowed him to experiment with editions and distribution through dealers such as George M. Beylerian and Charles Stendig.[3] Stendig also represented avant-garde Italian designers who specialized in these molded plastics, putting Castle in cutting-edge company.[4]

1. Gordon, *Wendell Castle: Wandering Forms*, 151–152 (images); Taragin et al., *Furniture by Wendell Castle*, 42.

2. Gordon, *Wendell Castle: Wandering Forms*, 140.

3. Ibid.; Taragin et al., *Furniture by Wendell Castle*, 42.

4. Gordon, *Wendell Castle: Wandering Forms*, 140.

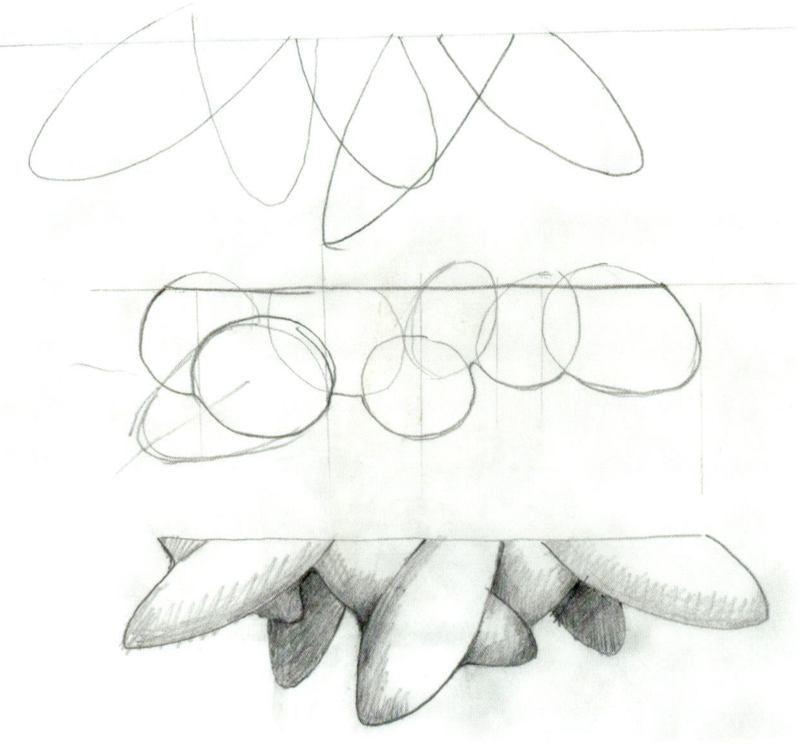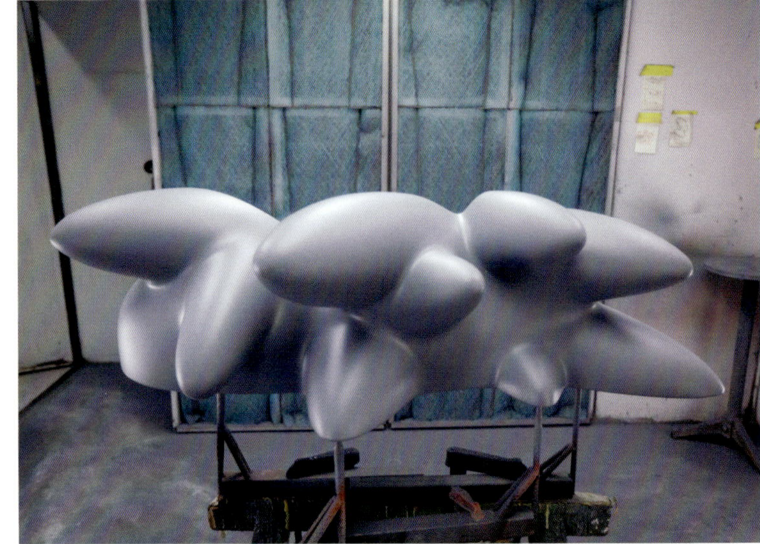

Plate 24

Cloud Shelf, 2015

Castle reinvigorates the whimsical *Cloud Shelf* from 1969 (plate 23) by reimagining it in relation to his contemporary vocabulary. A composition of bullet forms rather than the cartoon-esque interpretation of clouds in the earlier work, this new *Cloud Shelf* emanates an unsettling quality.

Environment for Contemplation, 1969–1970

In 1970, Paul J. Smith, former director of the Museum of Contemporary Crafts, organized the exhibition, *Contemplation Environments*, which explored physical spaces that encourage contemplation.[1] As his introduction to the exhibition catalogue states, "There can be said to exist a kind of ineffable presence in the architectural space itself which exerts a quieting, peaceful influence on the mind and emotions of the individual who enters it." Smith explains that traditionally such spaces were most frequently built as structures for worship, but Smith was interested in how people's "contemplative needs" were met in the busy, modern world.[2]

Castle, approached by Smith, created *Environment for Contemplation* expressly for the exhibition.[3] *Environment for Contemplation* received significant press coverage and inspired comparisons with a womb and a free-form coffin.[4] Castle, who frequently mentions his interest in automotive design, thought of his environment as a single-person vehicle with a trail of exhaust smoke languishing behind, which is clearly seen in the design.[5] A form that envelopes the sitter with padded, flokati-rug upholstery and darkness, pierced only from the light that enters through a small, porthole-like window in the ceiling, it is truly a product of its decade. *Environment for Contemplation* is part New-Age meditation cave, but also part soothing space where anyone can find some privacy with his or her thoughts, proving once again its relevance in today's increasingly "busy, modern world."

1. *Contemplation Environments* (New York: American Craftsmen's Council in association with the Museum of Contemporary Crafts), 3.

2. Ibid.

3. Gordon, *Wendell Castle: Wandering Forms*, 205.

4. Eerdmans, *Wendell Castle: A Catalogue Raisonné,* 78; Gordon, *Wendell Castle: Wandering Forms*, 205; Taragin et al., *Furniture by Wendell Castle*, 41.

5. Gordon, *Wendell Castle: Wandering Forms*, 205.

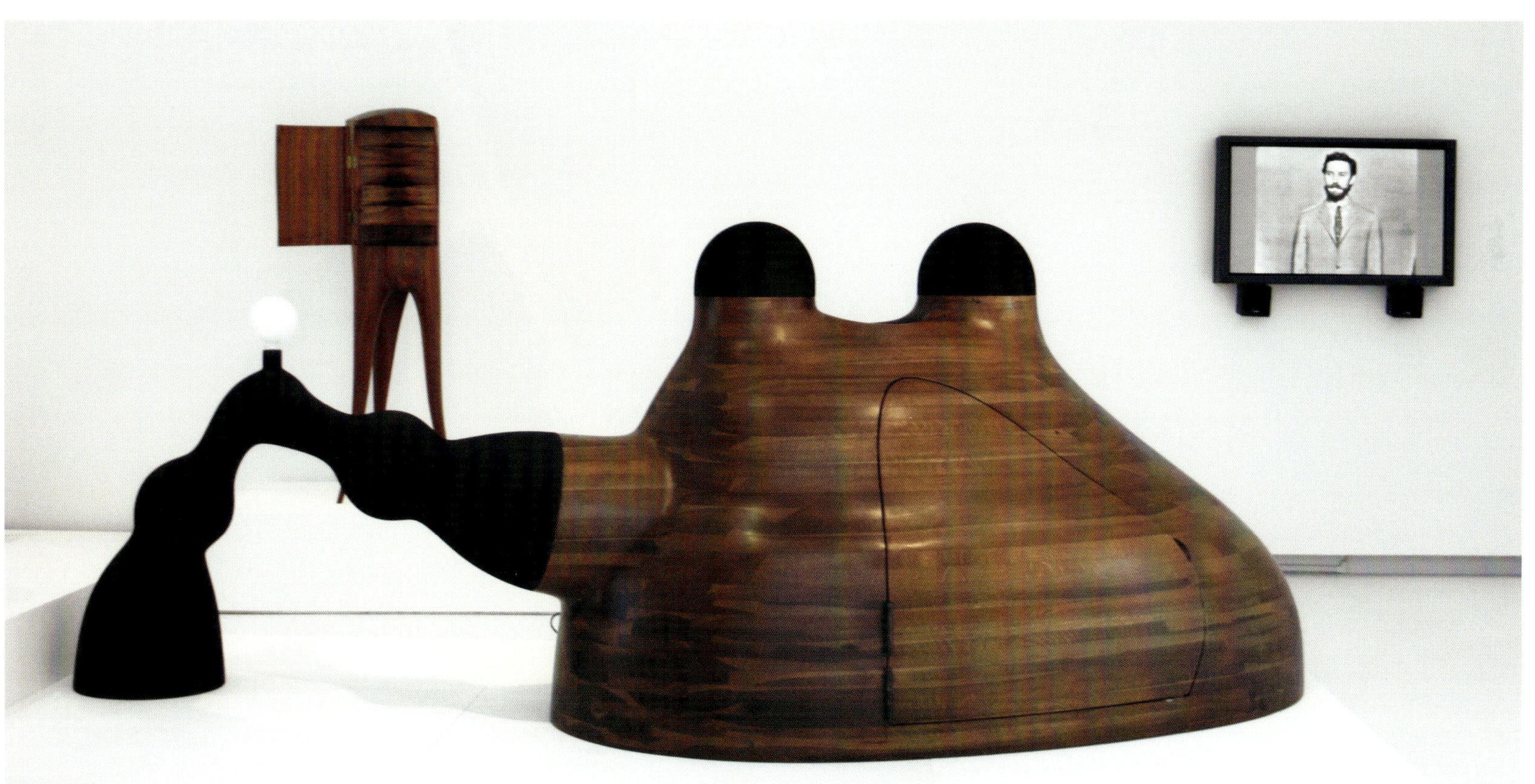

Plate 25

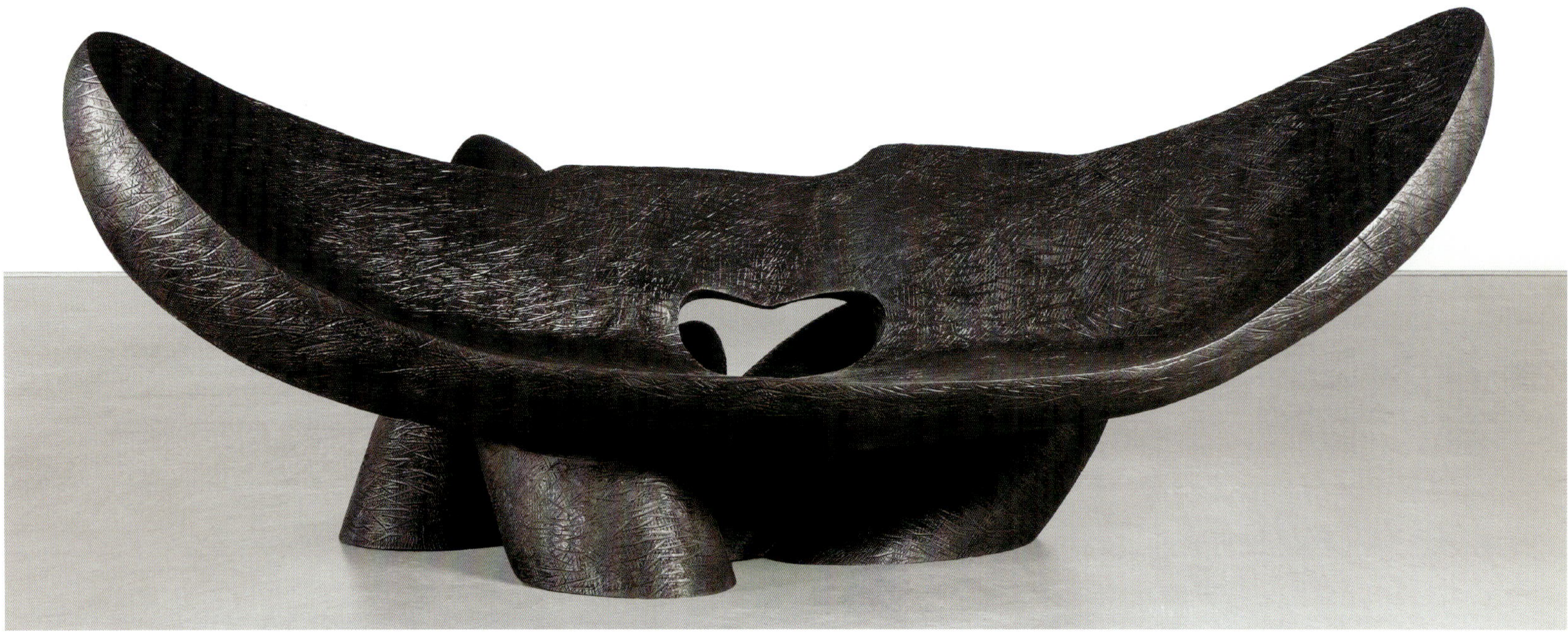

Plate 26 (front)

Temptation, 2014

Castle creates his new bronze works with the intention of both exterior and interior use. The hole in the seat of this mammoth sofa allows for drainage, indicating that it is conceived of as functional outdoor sculpture.

These cast-bronze sculptures are made in part at CWG Roissy, an "artisanal space" north of Paris, which was opened in 2014 by the Carpenters Workshop Gallery (CWG).[1] Only the metal-work is done outside of Castle's studio, however. Before that stage, Castle makes full-size plugs out of urethane foam that serve as the basis for a prototype, which can then be cast.[2] The Robot and its associated technology play a part here as well. The plug is made using the same stack-lamination techniques as the wooden pieces, rough-cut and carved by the Robot, and given a surface finish by hand.[3] Then, CWG makes a prototype based on this plug, commissions the casting out of house, and completes the surface finishing and refining to Castle's specifications.[4] The surface of *Temptation's* foam plug has been incised with repeating lines in a diagonal cross-hatch pattern, which will give the work a unique surface texture after casting.

1. Jean Rafferty, "Common Ground for Artists and Artisans," *New York Times* (March 26, 2015), accessed June 17, 2015, http://www. nytimes.com/2015/03/27/fashion/common-ground-for-artists-and-artisans.html?_r=0#.

2. Author's telephone interview with Castle, March 25, 2015.

3. Ibid.

4. Jean Rafferty, "Common Ground for Artists and Artisans."

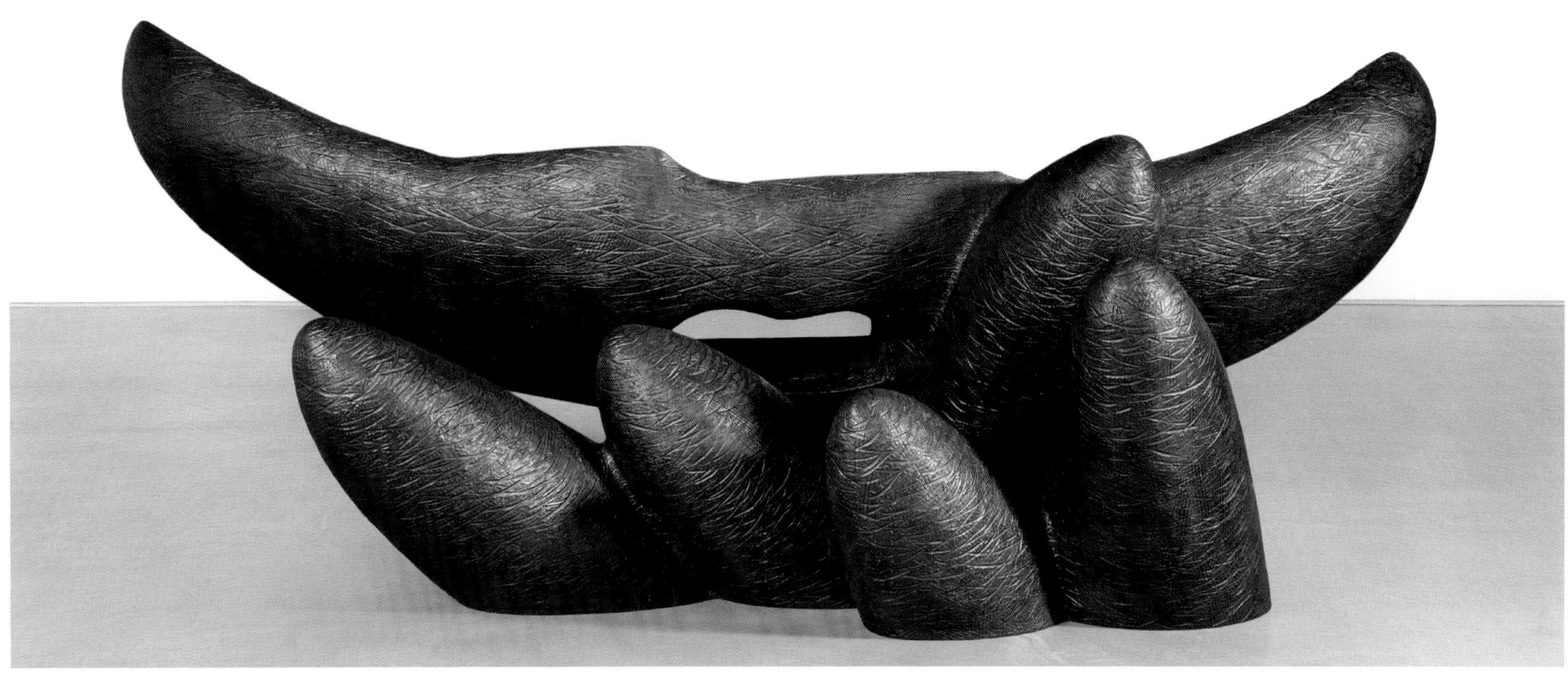

Plate 26 (back)

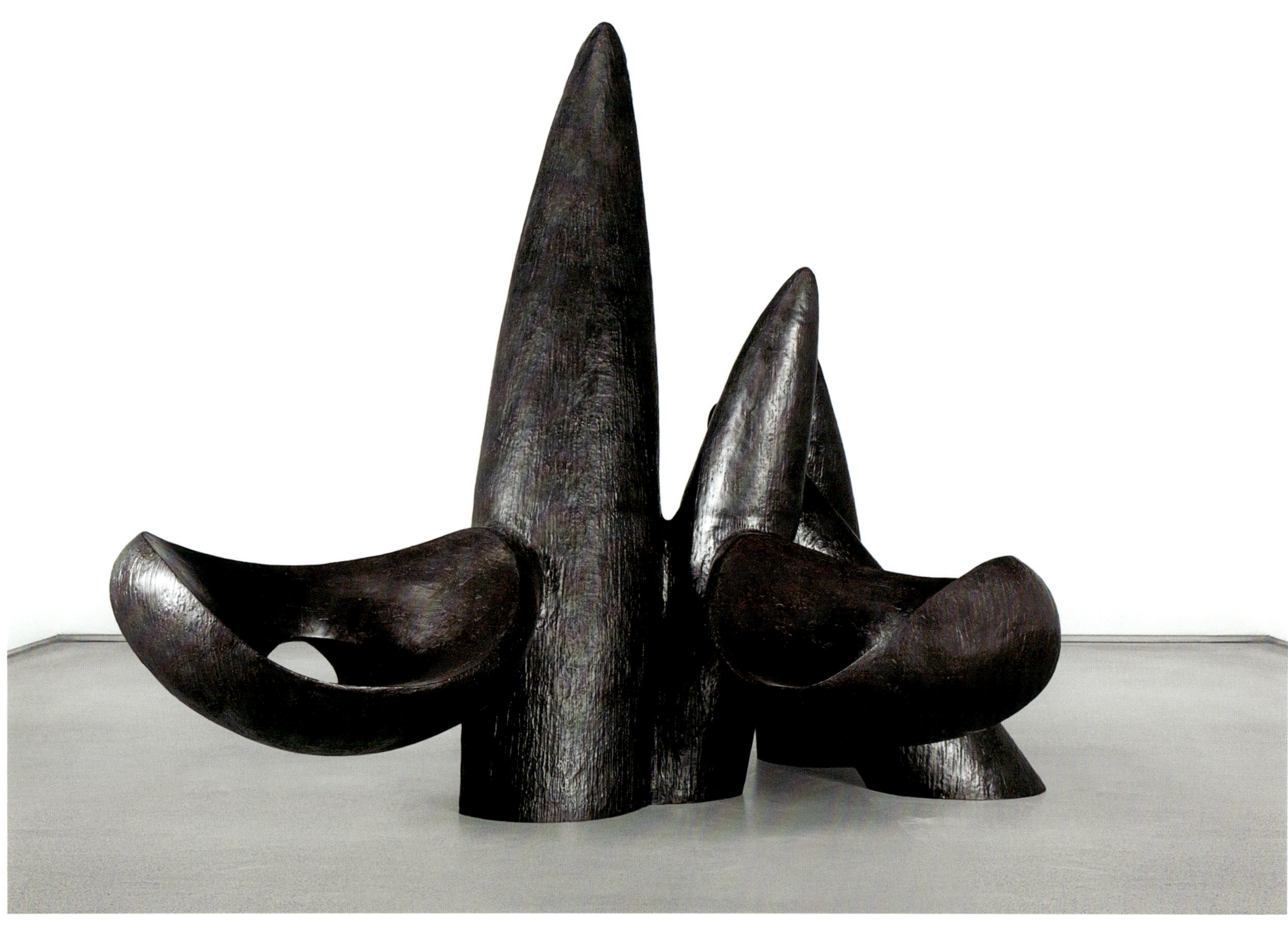

Plate 27

Wandering Mountain, 2014

Castle has long been interested in how his work can engage outdoor and public spaces.
Throughout his career, he has created such sculptures, including *M* (1971) for the Marine
Midland Bank in Rochester, New York; *Twist* (1972–1973), a public sculpture in Rochester;
and *Unicorn Family* (c. 2011), an outdoor living room installed at the Memorial Art Gallery,
University of Rochester, Rochester, New York.[1] He expands on an element of this type of
sculpture with his newest cast-bronze works, many of which are designed with outdoor use
in mind. The towering heights of *Wandering Mountain* make its presence imposing in a way
that creates the dynamism necessary for outdoor works, while the piercings in the seat allow
for rain and condensation to drain away

1. Gordon, *Wendell Castle: Wandering Forms*, 174, 181; Eerdmans,
Wendell Castle: A Catalogue Raisonné, 66, 425.

Like a Dream, 2014

Whimsical in design, *Like a Dream* is influenced by the classic cartoon trope of a single palm tree on a small island, on which someone invariably becomes marooned.[1] Originally influenced by "desert-island literature" of the eighteenth century—such as *Robinson Crusoe*—the desert-island cartoon has morphed over time from a detailed and realistic representation of a shipwreck scene to the greatly distilled icon of a single tree and tiny bit of land.[2] Castle took this trope and originally called it *Island Chair*.

Like a Dream is the answer to his musing, "Wouldn't it be nice if the person stranded on that island had a chair?"[3] So Castle created a chair—for that unfortunate castaway—that grows off of a stylized palm tree, the entirety on an organically shaped base that is an island of its own.[4]

1. Author's telephone interview with Castle, March 25, 2015; Bruce Handy, "A Guy, a Palm Tree, and a Desert Island: The Cartoon Genre That Just Won't Die," *Vanity Fair*, May 25, 2012, accessed March 30, 2015, http://www.vanityfair.com/culture/2012/05/history-of-the-desert-island-cartoon.

2. Bruce Handy, "A Guy, a Palm Tree, and a Desert Island."

3. Author's telephone interview with Castle, March 25, 2015.

4. Ibid.

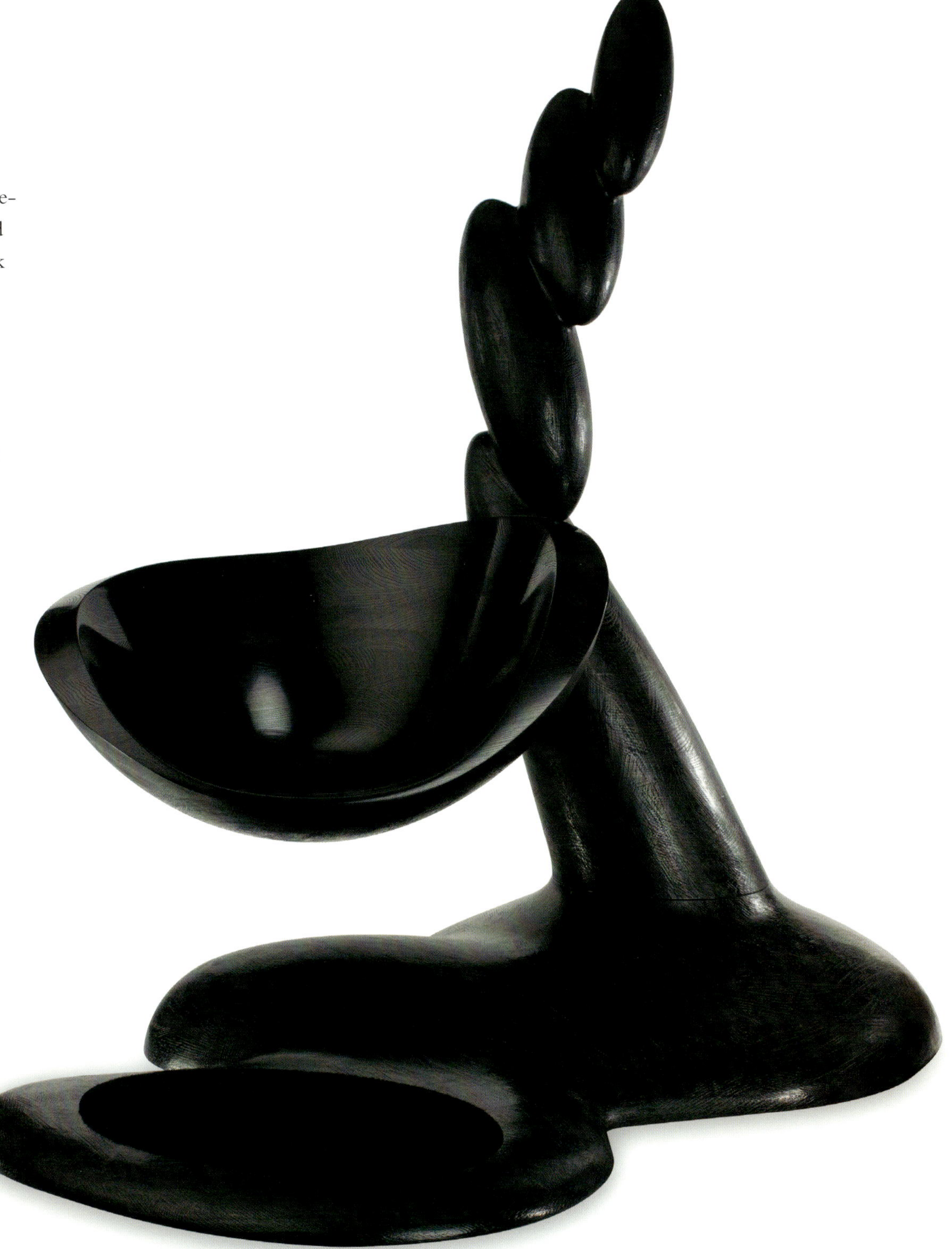

Plate 28

More or Less, 2014

As Castle continued to re-explore stack lamination, he began to expand upon his traditional vocabulary of forms—organically influenced combination furniture. One of these creative reimaginings led him to the thought, "What would happen if I grafted halves of two different chairs together?"[1] The result was Castle's self-titled "misfit" furniture, for which he does exactly that: he 3D scans two different chairs, digitally cuts them down the center, and recreates a chair comprised of half of each.[2] An example of this is *Crossroads* (fig. 5), a fully functional work; however, the seat does not line up entirely, creating a slightly off-beat aesthetic.

 More or Less is a precursor for these "misfit" chairs. Here, Castle simply created half a chair, extending the seat ever so slightly for the benefit of the sitter.[3] Its exposed cross section is slightly jarring when compared to the organic curves of the rest of Castle's work.

1. Author's telephone interview with Castle, March 25, 2015; Labaco and author's interview with Castle, Scottsville, NY, February 24, 2015.

2. Ibid.

3. Author's telephone interview with Castle, March 25, 2015.

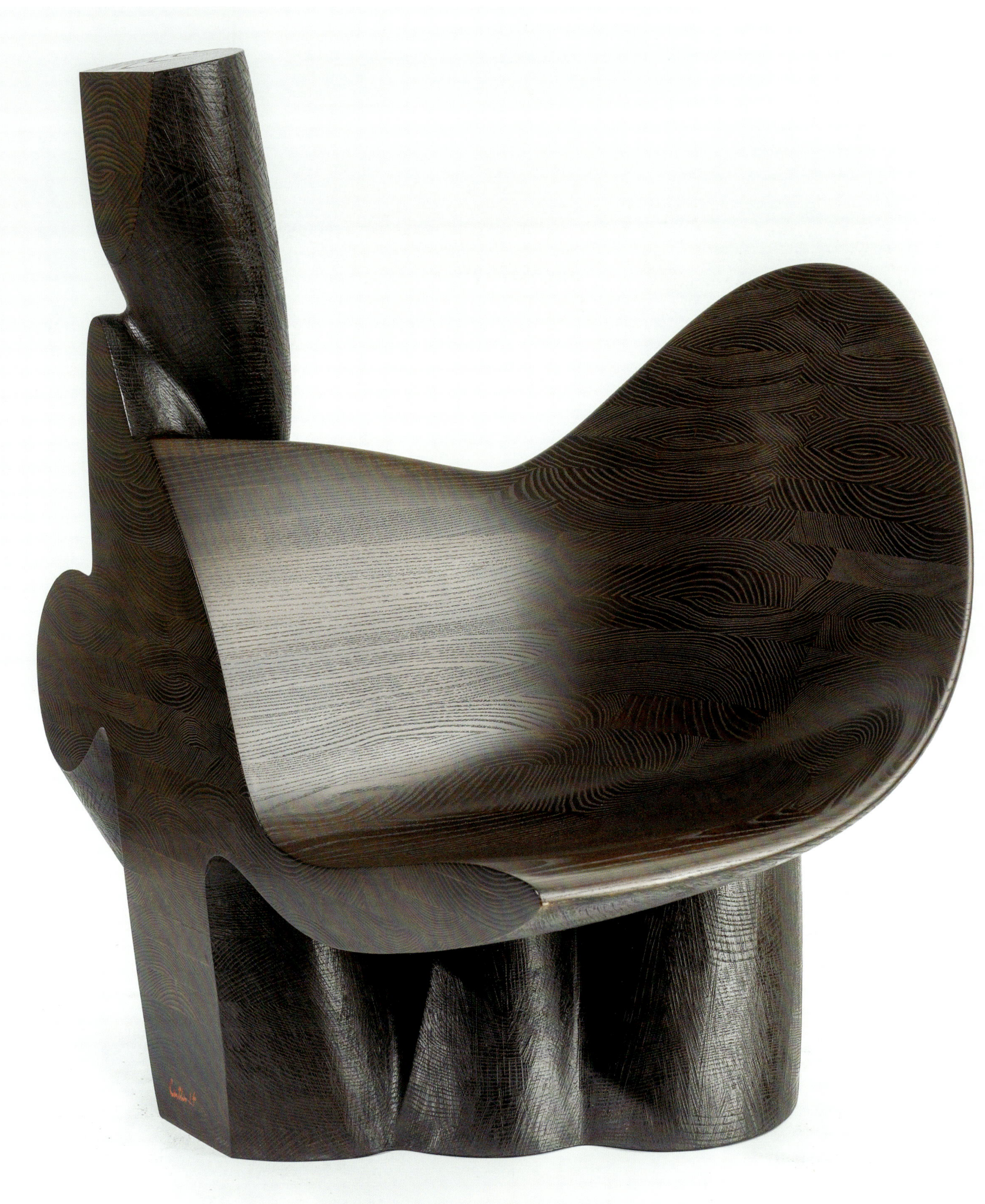

Plate 29

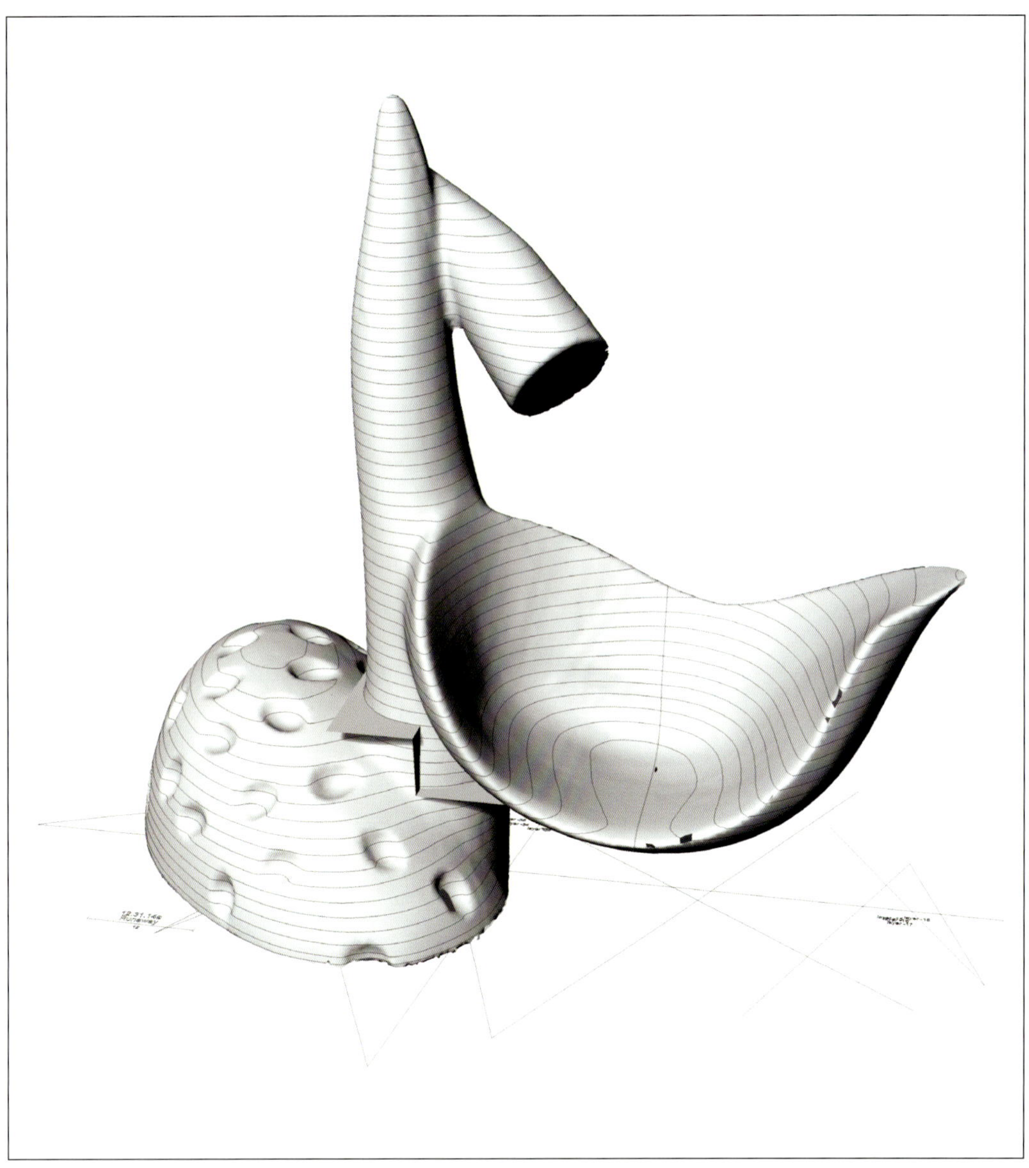

Plate 30

Runaway, 2015

For Castle, one of the most exciting aspects of the CNC milling robot is its ability to create a precise fit between two different organic forms that are combined.[1] Visualization of the complex connection is possible in the CAD model, and a series of preprogrammed steps and different-size bits allows the Robot to router a negative "mortise" in one and a positive "tenon" on the other, while creating a seamless fit between the two forms.[2] It is not possible to achieve this degree of exactness by hand. Loose tenons are then used to provide extra strength as well as to assure accurate alignment during assembly.

Runaway is comprised entirely of complex forms. Here, the seat and a lighting element both grow from a tentacle-like post, which itself seems to emerge from one of the holes in the biomorphic pod at the base.

1. Labaco and author's interview with Castle, Scottsville, NY, February 24, 2015; author's telephone interview with Castle, March 25, 2015; Labaco telephone interview with Castle, March 5, 2014.

2. Labaco and author's interview with Castle, Scottsville, NY, February 24, 2015.

Only What It Seems, 2011

The digital technologies Castle employs in his contemporary work—3D scanning, digital modeling, CNC-assisted carving—are tools to assist his still very much handcrafted work. Utilizing these tools does have its benefits, however, one of them being the computer's ability to store the RAPID code used to program it and recreate the same rough forms easily in order to make limited editions.[1] This, in turn, saves Castle from having to make multiples of the same work, which is not very practical or engaging, especially with the larger works. *Only What It Seems*, an edition of eight with two artist proofs and two prototypes, is an excellent example of the benefit of the Robot.

1. Author's telephone interview with Castle, March 25, 2015; Labaco telephone interview with Pallischeck, August 1, 2014; Sims interview with Castle, Scottsville, NY, March 24, 2015; Cheatle and Jackson, "Digital Entanglements: Craft, Computation and Collaboration in Fine Arts Furniture Production," 5.

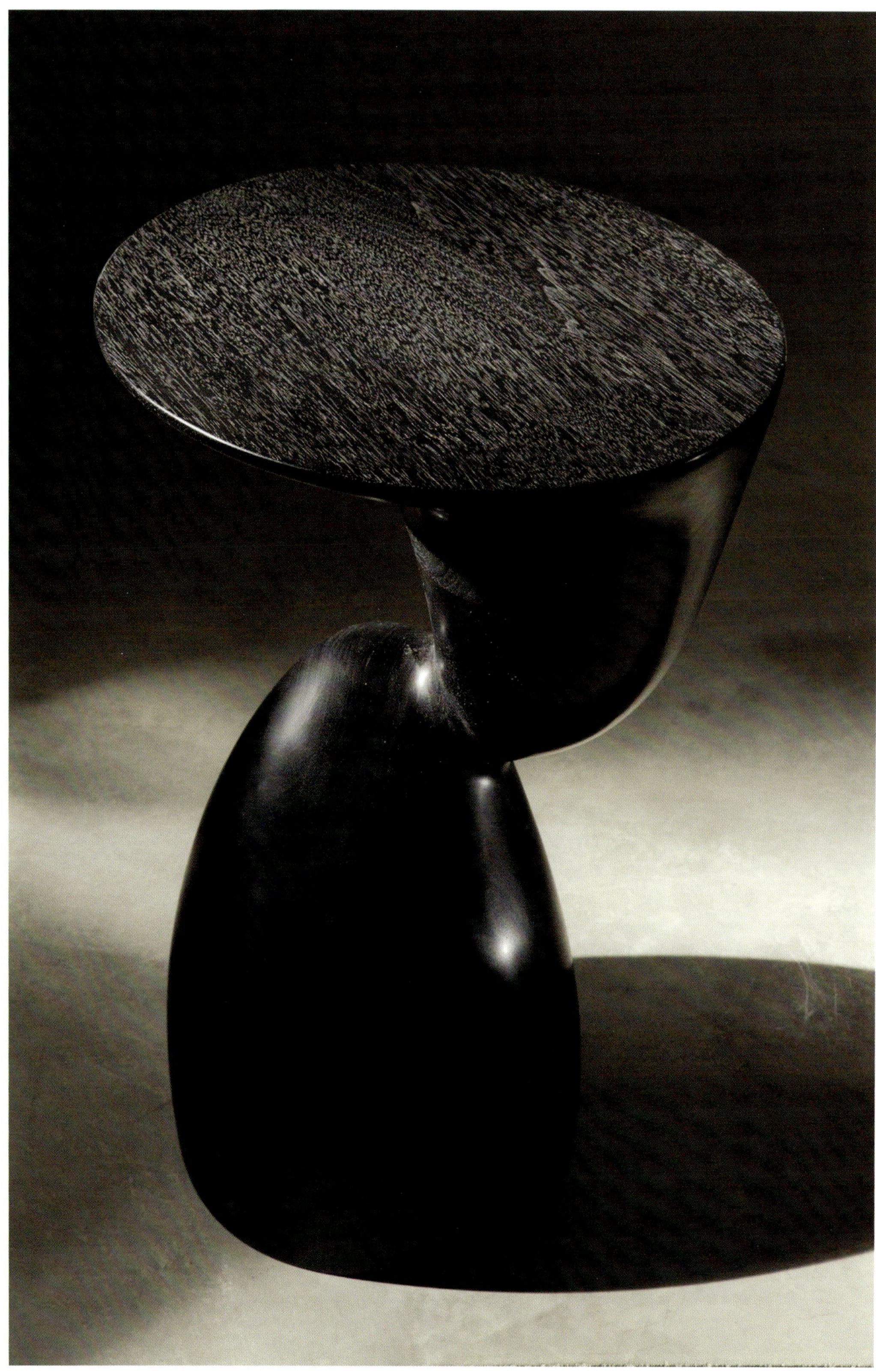

Plate 31

```
LANGUAGE:ENGLISH
%%%

MODULE Long Night
  !CONST zonedata z0:=[FALSE,1,1,1,1,1,1];
  PERS tooldata t1:=[TRUE,[[434.34,0,109.73],[0.7071068,0,0.7071068,0]],[23,[0,0,100],[1,0,0,0],0.01,0.01,0.01]];
  PERS wobjdata w1:=[FALSE,TRUE,"",[[1714.5,0,285.24],[1,0,0,0]],[[0,0,0],[1,0,0,0]]];

  PROC main()
    MoveAbsJ [[12.791,22.732,22.004,31.213,-25.291,-28.717],[9E+9,9E+9,9E+9,9E+9,9E+9,9E+9]],v100,fine,t1;
    MoveL [[369.533,402.808,817.237],[0,0,1,0],[0,0,-1,0],[9E+9,9E+9,9E+9,9E+9,9E+9,9E+9]],v300,z0,t1\WObj:=w1;
    MoveL [[369.533,402.808,667.899],[0,0,1,0],[0,0,-1,0],[9E+9,9E+9,9E+9,9E+9,9E+9,9E+9]],v150,z0,t1\WObj:=w1;
    MoveL [[369.533,402.808,661.549],[0,0,1,0],[0,0,-1,0],[9E+9,9E+9,9E+9,9E+9,9E+9,9E+9]],v150,z0,t1\WObj:=w1;
    MoveL [[369.533,404.416,653.889],[0,0,1,0],[0,0,-1,0],[9E+9,9E+9,9E+9,9E+9,9E+9,9E+9]],v150,z0,t1\WObj:=w1;
    MoveL [[369.533,408.969,647.522],[0,0,1,0],[0,0,-1,0],[9E+9,9E+9,9E+9,9E+9,9E+9,9E+9]],v150,z0,t1\WObj:=w1;
    MoveL [[369.533,408.969,817.237],[0,0,1,0],[0,0,-1,0],[9E+9,9E+9,9E+9,9E+9,9E+9,9E+9]],v300,z0,t1\WObj:=w1;
    MoveL [[-167.494,-188.362,817.237],[0,0,1,0],[-1,-1,0,0],[9E+9,9E+9,9E+9,9E+9,9E+9,9E+9]],v300,z0,t1\WObj:=w1;
    MoveL [[-167.494,-188.362,642.084],[0,0,1,0],[-1,-1,0,0],[9E+9,9E+9,9E+9,9E+9,9E+9,9E+9]],v150,z0,t1\WObj:=w1;
    MoveL [[-167.494,-188.362,635.734],[0,0,1,0],[-1,-1,0,0],[9E+9,9E+9,9E+9,9E+9,9E+9,9E+9]],v150,z0,t1\WObj:=w1;
    MoveL [[-170.272,-183.454,622.203],[0,0,1,0],[-1,-1,0,0],[9E+9,9E+9,9E+9,9E+9,9E+9,9E+9]],v150,z0,t1\WObj:=w1;
    MoveL [[-176.961,-171.635,616.684],[0,0,1,0],[-1,-1,0,0],[9E+9,9E+9,9E+9,9E+9,9E+9,9E+9]],v150,z0,t1\WObj:=w1;
    MoveL [[-178.541,-168.842,616.788],[0,0,1,0],[-1,-1,0,0],[9E+9,9E+9,9E+9,9E+9,9E+9,9E+9]],v150,z0,t1\WObj:=w1;
    MoveL [[-180.554,-165.286,616.674],[0,0,1,0],[-1,-1,0,0],[9E+9,9E+9,9E+9,9E+9,9E+9,9E+9]],v150,z0,t1\WObj:=w1;
    MoveL [[-182.567,-161.73,616.386],[0,0,1,0],[-1,-1,0,0],[9E+9,9E+9,9E+9,9E+9,9E+9,9E+9]],v150,z0,t1\WObj:=w1;
    MoveL [[-184.579,-158.174,616.36],[0,0,1,0],[-1,-1,0,0],[9E+9,9E+9,9E+9,9E+9,9E+9,9E+9]],v150,z0,t1\WObj:=w1;
    MoveL [[-186.592,-154.618,616.175],[0,0,1,0],[-1,-1,0,0],[9E+9,9E+9,9E+9,9E+9,9E+9,9E+9]],v150,z0,t1\WObj:=w1;
    MoveL [[-188.539,-151.177,616.111],[0,0,1,0],[-1,-1,0,0],[9E+9,9E+9,9E+9,9E+9,9E+9,9E+9]],v150,z0,t1\WObj:=w1;
    MoveL [[-190.91,-146.988,615.88],[0,0,1,0],[-1,-1,0,0],[9E+9,9E+9,9E+9,9E+9,9E+9,9E+9]],v150,z0,t1\WObj:=w1;
    MoveL [[-192.629,-143.95,615.686],[0,0,1,0],[-1,-1,0,0],[9E+9,9E+9,9E+9,9E+9,9E+9,9E+9]],v150,z0,t1\WObj:=w1;
    MoveL [[-194.642,-140.394,615.535],[0,0,1,0],[-1,-1,0,0],[9E+9,9E+9,9E+9,9E+9,9E+9,9E+9]],v150,z0,t1\WObj:=w1;
    MoveL [[-196.654,-136.838,615.362],[0,0,1,0],[-1,-1,0,0],[9E+9,9E+9,9E+9,9E+9,9E+9,9E+9]],v150,z0,t1\WObj:=w1;
    MoveL [[-198.667,-133.282,615.155],[0,0,1,0],[-1,-1,0,0],[9E+9,9E+9,9E+9,9E+9,9E+9,9E+9]],v150,z0,t1\WObj:=w1;
    MoveL [[-200.679,-129.726,614.957],[0,0,1,0],[-1,-1,0,0],[9E+9,9E+9,9E+9,9E+9,9E+9,9E+9]],v150,z0,t1\WObj:=w1;
    MoveL [[-202.692,-126.17,614.726],[0,0,1,0],[-1,-1,0,0],[9E+9,9E+9,9E+9,9E+9,9E+9,9E+9]],v150,z0,t1\WObj:=w1;
    MoveL [[-204.705,-122.614,614.353],[0,0,1,0],[-1,-1,0,0],[9E+9,9E+9,9E+9,9E+9,9E+9,9E+9]],v150,z0,t1\WObj:=w1;
    MoveL [[-206.319,-119.8,614.205],[0,0,1,0],[-1,-1,0,0],[9E+9,9E+9,9E+9,9E+9,9E+9,9E+9]],v150,z0,t1\WObj:=w1;
    MoveL [[-208.403,-116.687,613.767],[0,0,1,0],[-1,-1,0,0],[9E+9,9E+9,9E+9,9E+9,9E+9,9E+9]],v150,z0,t1\WObj:=w1;
    MoveL [[-212.246,-110.949,612.93],[0,0,1,0],[-1,-1,0,0],[9E+9,9E+9,9E+9,9E+9,9E+9,9E+9]],v150,z0,t1\WObj:=w1;
    MoveL [[-214.753,-107.204,612.393],[0,0,1,0],[-1,-1,0,0],[9E+9,9E+9,9E+9,9E+9,9E+9,9E+9]],v150,z0,t1\WObj:=w1;
    MoveL [[-217.134,-103.648,612.187],[0,0,1,0],[-1,-1,0,0],[9E+9,9E+9,9E+9,9E+9,9E+9,9E+9]],v150,z0,t1\WObj:=w1;
    MoveL [[-219.358,-100.328,611.956],[0,0,1,0],[-1,-1,0,0],[9E+9,9E+9,9E+9,9E+9,9E+9,9E+9]],v150,z0,t1\WObj:=w1;
    MoveL [[-221.103,-97.722,612.064],[0,0,1,0],[-1,-1,0,0],[9E+9,9E+9,9E+9,9E+9,9E+9,9E+9]],v150,z0,t1\WObj:=w1;
    MoveL [[-222.914,-95.094,612.481],[0,0,1,0],[-1,-1,0,0],[9E+9,9E+9,9E+9,9E+9,9E+9,9E+9]],v150,z0,t1\WObj:=w1;
    MoveL [[-225.284,-92.358,612.372],[0,0,1,0],[-1,-1,0,0],[9E+9,9E+9,9E+9,9E+9,9E+9,9E+9]],v150,z0,t1\WObj:=w1;
    MoveL [[-227.655,-89.691,612.545],[0,0,1,0],[-1,-1,0,0],[9E+9,9E+9,9E+9,9E+9,9E+9,9E+9]],v150,z0,t1\WObj:=w1;
    MoveL [[-230.026,-87.614,612.667],[0,0,1,0],[-1,-1,0,0],[9E+9,9E+9,9E+9,9E+9,9E+9,9E+9]],v150,z0,t1\WObj:=w1;
    MoveL [[-232.396,-85.537,612.849],[0,0,1,0],[-1,-1,0,0],[9E+9,9E+9,9E+9,9E+9,9E+9,9E+9]],v150,z0,t1\WObj:=w1;
    MoveL [[-234.723,-83.498,613.78],[0,0,1,0],[-1,-1,0,0],[9E+9,9E+9,9E+9,9E+9,9E+9,9E+9]],v150,z0,t1\WObj:=w1;

    MoveL [[324.457,-119.058,711.251],[0,0,1,0],[-1,-1,0,0],[9E+9,9E+9,9E+9,9E+9,9E+9,9E+9]],v150,z0,t1\WObj:=w1;
    MoveL [[323.525,-122.008,710.745],[0,0,1,0],[-1,-1,0,0],[9E+9,9E+9,9E+9,9E+9,9E+9,9E+9]],v150,z0,t1\WObj:=w1;
    MoveL [[322.613,-124.984,710.201],[0,0,1,0],[-1,-1,0,0],[9E+9,9E+9,9E+9,9E+9,9E+9,9E+9]],v150,z0,t1\WObj:=w1;
    MoveL [[321.567,-128.54,709.535],[0,0,1,0],[-1,-1,0,0],[9E+9,9E+9,9E+9,9E+9,9E+9,9E+9]],v150,z0,t1\WObj:=w1;
    MoveL [[320.557,-132.096,708.853],[0,0,1,0],[-1,-1,0,0],[9E+9,9E+9,9E+9,9E+9,9E+9,9E+9]],v150,z0,t1\WObj:=w1;
    MoveL [[319.541,-135.652,708.145],[0,0,1,0],[-1,-1,0,0],[9E+9,9E+9,9E+9,9E+9,9E+9,9E+9]],v150,z0,t1\WObj:=w1;
    MoveL [[318.482,-139.208,707.426],[0,0,1,0],[-1,-1,0,0],[9E+9,9E+9,9E+9,9E+9,9E+9,9E+9]],v150,z0,t1\WObj:=w1;
    MoveL [[317.598,-142.051,706.814],[0,0,1,0],[-1,-1,0,0],[9E+9,9E+9,9E+9,9E+9,9E+9,9E+9]],v150,z0,t1\WObj:=w1;
    MoveL [[316.654,-145.135,706.14],[0,0,1,0],[-1,-1,0,0],[9E+9,9E+9,9E+9,9E+9,9E+9,9E+9]],v150,z0,t1\WObj:=w1;
    MoveL [[315.512,-148.691,705.383],[0,0,1,0],[-1,-1,0,0],[9E+9,9E+9,9E+9,9E+9,9E+9,9E+9]],v150,z0,t1\WObj:=w1;
    MoveL [[314.293,-152.247,704.56],[0,0,1,0],[-1,-1,0,0],[9E+9,9E+9,9E+9,9E+9,9E+9,9E+9]],v150,z0,t1\WObj:=w1;
    MoveL [[314.293,-152.247,804.560],[0,0,1,0],[-1,-1,0,0],[9E+9,9E+9,9E+9,9E+9,9E+9,9E+9]],v150,z0,t1\WObj:=w1;
  ENDPROC
ENDMODULE
```

Digital Entanglements

AMY CHEATLE AND STEVEN J. JACKSON

CONTEMPORARY RESEARCH IN TECHNOLOGY STUDIES and human–computer interaction has sought to examine, in newly expansive ways, the relationship between creative practices and the material tools and infrastructures that frame and support them. Reading across creative communities from science and politics to music and the arts, this body of work has produced a number of core findings: that tools are rarely just tools; that changes in infrastructure can produce changes in human value; that computational objects may be deeply embedded in the pleasure and possibility of work, both individual and collective; and that the worlds of objects and people may be less far apart than commonly imagined. This has unique implications, particularly for how we might shift popular notions of artists' and designers' roles toward what anthropologist Tim Ingold has characterized as a kind of "wayfarer" who brings forth work by gathering and bending the material flows and trajectories that surround them.[1] These findings also bear on how we imagine creativity itself, as practiced in a world of intersecting human and nonhuman agents, or, as argued elsewhere, "creativity is something we do in and with the world, not just to it."[2]

This essay shares our experiences in Wendell Castle's studio, which we visited over the spring and summer of 2014 as part of a larger series of studies on how computational development has impacted patterns of value, innovation, and collaboration across a range of creative fields.[3] As the work in this exhibition, *Wendell Castle Remastered*, makes clear, the Castle studio has long been at the forefront of the American art-furniture movement, which is defined in part by a design practice grounded in experimental tool use and adventurous problem solving. This practice has evolved alongside Castle's work since the first days of his pioneering use of the stack-lamination process to achieve new scales and unities of form. In some ways, Castle's recent turn to complex computational tools represents simply the next step in a career-long trajectory of innovation driven by his ongoing quest to "free wood from its material constraints."[4] In others, it marks a turning point in his creative process, made powerful through a new suite of contemporary tools more frequently found in manufacturing environments. We argue here that the studio's collaborative use of crafting technologies, the material properties of wood, and Castle's own conceptual and imaginative practices have been expanded and reworked through the integration of complex computational tools and systems. At the same time, the collaborative work of the wider studio team has been reconfigured, generating new, technologically oriented roles while extending or altering others that are more traditional. By focusing on the collaborative process that brings a Castle piece into being, we can begin to understand how these tools have, in his words, "freed up" the design from some of its material constraints, leading to new formal, practical, and creative possibilities.

The sections below trace the contemporary work practices of the Castle studio by focusing on two central questions: How has the integration of complex computational design tools and manufacturing robotics maintained or expanded Castle's conceptual and imaginative practices? And how have collaborations in the studio been remixed as a result of these new tools? To tell our story, we follow one work, Castle's chair, *Long Night* (plate 5), as it traverses the worlds of imagination, teamwork, and tool use that constitute his studio practice. While following the studio's process, we pay particular attention to the introduction of 3D scanning and laminate template printing, as well as the studio's recent adoption of a computer-numerical-control (CNC) machine sourced from the U.S. Postal Service.

Before the demand for his work sparked the studio's growth and the hiring of additional artisans to assist with some of the work, Castle performed each step of the process described below. Historically, he began each piece with a series of small pencil drawings. One sketch would be placed on an opaque projector where it was beamed and then traced onto a large sheet of paper to which Castle could add lamination guides (cross sections). As the studio grew to include artisan assistants, both the full-scale drawing and earlier sketches would be given to them to use as guides that would help shape the process. Using the drawings, Castle or his assistants would cut planks of wood that they then stacked, glued, and clamped into a rough shape, and then further refined using a series of hand tools (including the chainsaw). The fine art piece as conceptualized by Castle would then be refined and completed with the relevant hand detailing and finishing treatments. The drawings accompanied the object through every aspect of the design, traversing the project's stages through the capable hands of Castle or his studio artisans.

However revolutionary this process might seem to those studying the collaborative studio practices of a fine art furniture maker, in Castle's thinking it presented challenges and limitations that constricted his design potentials. As he explained, the cross sections he drew on the large sketch were informally imagined rather than precisely mapped, and this estimation could result not only in frustrations but also in the loss of time, energy, and material. In Castle's words, "We absolutely needed to work in a different way. We needed to get an accurate model of these cross sections. If we glued up the pieces accurately, it would greatly reduce carving."[5] In addition, the method of carving the stack laminate posed significant challenges to the successful completion of the work, as Castle found that not all woodworkers could "see" and "find" the final form of the work in the rough stack. "Carvers know how to be reductive to reveal the final form, and then know when to stop. They somehow see 'it' in their minds."[6] Traditionally trained woodworkers, while familiar with wood's physical opportunities and constraints, may not experience positive and negative space in the same way a sculptor or carver does. While the printed patterns helped to guide the carver, Castle wanted to realize his forms with higher degrees of accuracy and speed. This drove his experimentation with technological tools and created a cutting-edge design process that for the past five years has expanded both his practice and the resulting creative-design objects he brings forth.

During our observational work in the Castle studio, we witnessed a team of highly skilled craftsmen engaged in a process rich with both computational—as well as more traditionally artisanal—tools. The team was nearing the final stages of adopting "the Robot," a six-axis, computer-numerical-control (CNC) machine tool that resembles a large mechanical arm with a router attached at its end, driven by a computer program and meant to replace the carver and his chainsaw during the rough cut of the stack laminate. The CNC was another digital integration into a complex studio process that had already evolved to include computer-aided-design (CAD) tools more frequently found in the industrial design and manufacturing fields. The studio was about to begin an edition of *Long Night*, originally developed by hand as a one-off object for Castle's 2011 exhibition, *Best Leg Forward*. We traced the formation of this edition of nearly identical pieces, as they marked the studio's first explorations into the use of CNC. Castle believed the Robot might help the studio carvers with some of the repetitive "grunt" work, while potentially improving the speed and accuracy of the first cuts, thus enabling an edition of *Long Night* to come into being in a timely and precise manner.

The original *Long Night* was shipped by the Carpenters Workshop Gallery in Paris, France, back to the Castle studio in upstate New York, where a portable, handheld scanning wand enabled computational technicians to render the fine art object into a digital CAD model. Then, accurate laminate demarcation lines were applied to this digital model resulting in the formation of individual patterns that could be printed as large paper shapes that would guide the creation of the stacked-wood layers. As the wood planks were cut and stacked by the studio's craftsmen, Marvin Pallischeck—Castle's studio manager as well as the computational programmer and technician—translated the CAD drawing into a set of CAM (computer-aided manufacturing) G and M codes used to drive and direct CNC machines with a software tool called Rhinocam. Next, the Rhinocam file was translated again, this time into hundreds of thousands of lines of RAPID code, the proprietary software language read by the studio's specific CNC machine, guiding the rough cuts made to the laminate stack. On the process of driving the CNC machine, Pallischeck said, "It's an act of faith. You hit that go button and you hope you haven't made a mistake somewhere."[7] The Robot, moving at two meters a second, was mesmerizing to watch. It quickly milled the laminate stack as programmed, revealing *Long Night* in rough cut. Once milled, the studio could resume its traditional practice of passing the piece off to its artisans who skillfully adjusted and finished the final surface of the work. In this way, each piece would end with the meticulous handwork of the finishing craftsmen.

It took Pallischeck over a year to adapt the robotic carving arm for studio use. Once integrated into the work flow, the impact of such a new tool was felt by the studio carvers in several ways. The CNC machine finished carving an object at an incredible pace, reducing the amount of time and physical labor previously needed to craft a Castle design. The carving arm, when programmed properly, could "see" the form in ways that so many studio carvers had struggled with in the past. In addition, the code used to drive the CNC could be reused on subsequent pieces, reducing the redundancy of studio-carving labor, thereby eliminating some of the grunt work from carvers tasked with forging editions, or multiples, of an object.

Perhaps more powerfully, an unanticipated affordance resulted from the use of the carving arm and it stemmed from the machine's extended reach. The Robot was capable of reaching underneath, around, and within the wood block, forming a sculpture in ways a human arm and chainsaw could not. This extended reach opened Castle's designs to new sculptural possibilities. The Robot's reach also allowed for previously challenging joinery to be realized in a practical and timely fashion. Responding to this, Castle began to create larger and more complex works than were previously possible. As he explained, the CNC robot had "freed up the vocabulary" of his design, thereby allowing his creative and conceptual work to expand in formerly impossible ways. Despite affordances and

1. Every Castle design begins with a sketch. Numerous sketches showing various Castle designs collect on walls and tabletops throughout the studio.

2. This is a screenshot of the digital model of *Long Night* (plate 5) as seen in the computer-aided-design (CAD) software, Rhinoceros (Rhino). Here, the cross sections have been added to indicate layers of lamination.

3. This printout of a Rhino digital model illustrates the layers of lamination that will be glued together to create the rough form of an artwork.

4. Here, Marvin Pallischeck, Castle's studio manager and computational programmer and technician, manipulates digital models in Rhino. He makes any adjustments to the design indicated by Castle, creates cross sections to indicate layers of lamination, and finalizes the scale.

5. The digital model is then rendered—using the computer-aided-manufacturing (CAM) software, Rhinocam—into hundreds of thousands of lines of RAPID code, a programming language that the computer-numerical-control (CNC) machine can read. This code will drive the CNC machine as it mills the rough stack-laminated form to match Castle's design.

6. Here, a full-scale paper pattern for one of the laminate layers can be seen; this is known as a cross section. Each cross section forms a unique layer and is derived from the 3D digital model generated in Rhino. These cross sections act as templates and are traced by hand onto the wooden boards to be cut out on the band saw.

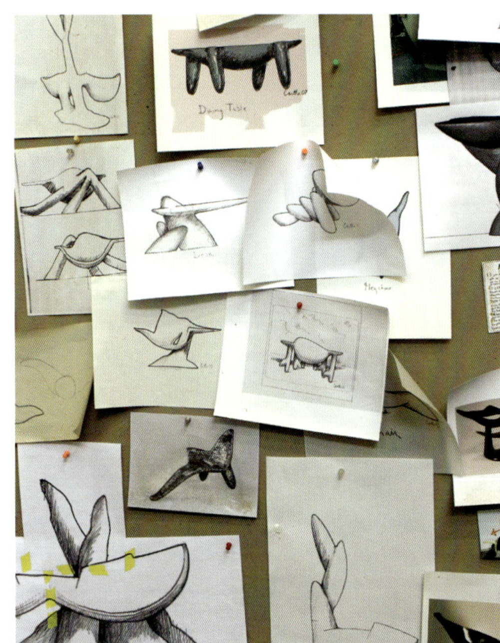

1.

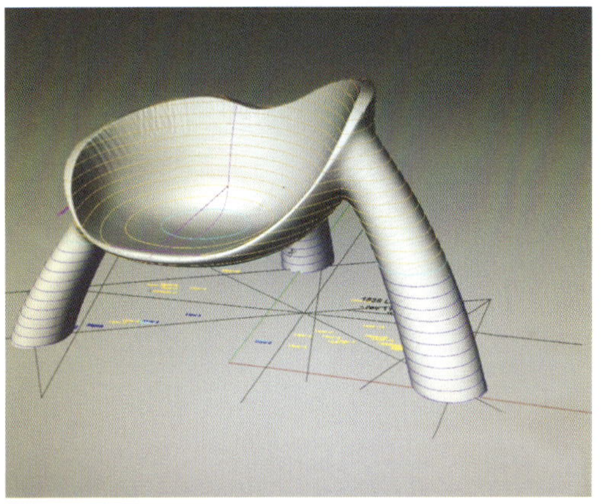

2.

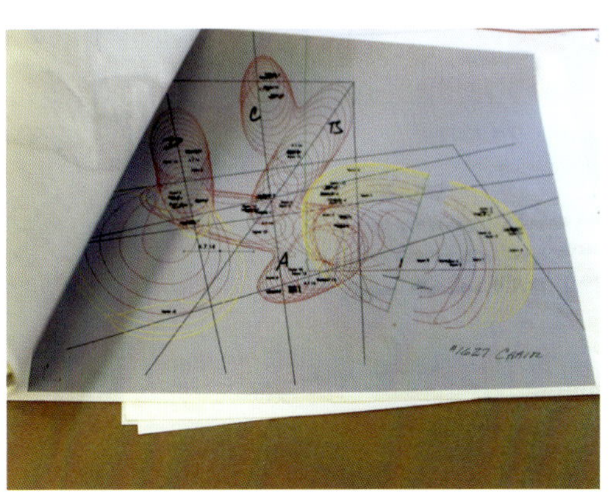

3.

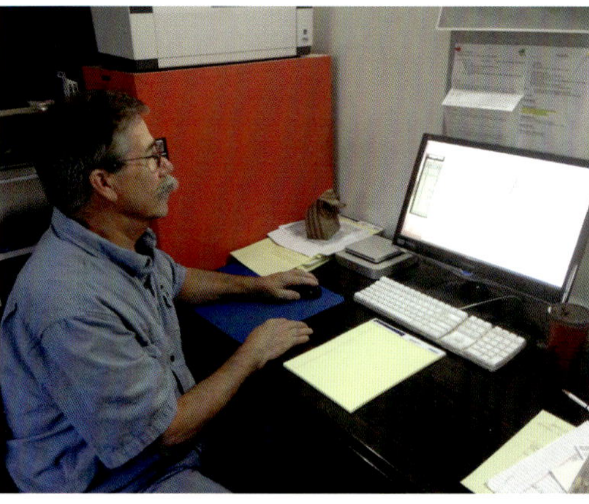

4.

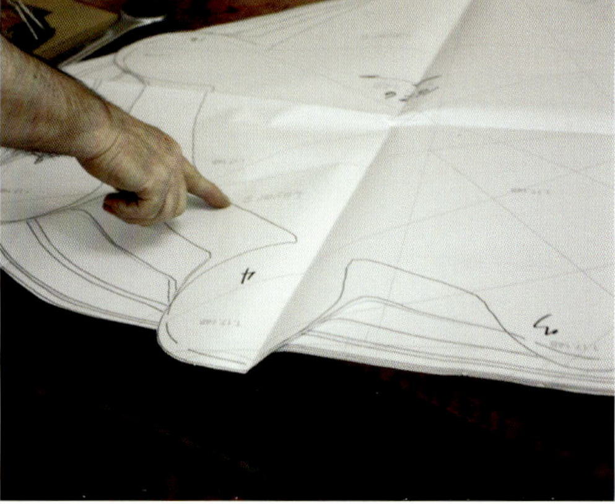

369.533,402.808,817.237],[0,0,1,0],[0,0,-1,0],[9E+9,9E+9,9E+9,9E+9,9E+9,9E+9
369.533,402.808,667.899],[0,0,1,0],[0,0,-1,0],[9E+9,9E+9,9E+9,9E+9,9E+9,9E+9
369.533,402.808,661.549],[0,0,1,0],[0,0,-1,0],[9E+9,9E+9,9E+9,9E+9,9E+9,9E+9
369.533,404.416,653.889],[0,0,1,0],[0,0,-1,0],[9E+9,9E+9,9E+9,9E+9,9E+9,9E+9
369.533,408.969,647.522],[0,0,1,0],[0,0,-1,0],[9E+9,9E+9,9E+9,9E+9,9E+9,9E+9
369.533,408.969,817.237],[0,0,1,0],[0,0,-1,0],[9E+9,9E+9,9E+9,9E+9,9E+9,9E+9
-167.494,-188.362,817.237],[0,0,1,0],[-1,-1,0,0],[9E+9,9E+9,9E+9,9E+9,9E+9,9
-167.494,-188.362,642.084],[0,0,1,0],[-1,-1,0,0],[9E+9,9E+9,9E+9,9E+9,9E+9,9
-167.494,-188.362,635.734],[0,0,1,0],[-1,-1,0,0],[9E+9,9E+9,9E+9,9E+9,9E+9,9
-170.272,-183.454,622.203],[0,0,1,0],[-1,-1,0,0],[9E+9,9E+9,9E+9,9E+9,9E+9,9
-176.961,-171.635,616.684],[0,0,1,0],[-1,-1,0,0],[9E+9,9E+9,9E+9,9E+9,9E+9,9
-178.541,-168.842,616.788],[0,0,1,0],[-1,-1,0,0],[9E+9,9E+9,9E+9,9E+9,9E+9,9
-180.554,-165.286,616.674],[0,0,1,0],[-1,-1,0,0],[9E+9,9E+9,9E+9,9E+9,9E+9,9
-182.567,-161.73,616.386],[0,0,1,0],[-1,-1,0,0],[9E+9,9E+9,9E+9,9E+9,9E+9,9E
-184.579,-158.174,616.36],[0,0,1,0],[-1,-1,0,0],[9E+9,9E+9,9E+9,9E+9,9E+9,9E
-186.592,-154.618,616.175],[0,0,1,0],[-1,-1,0,0],[9E+9,9E+9,9E+9,9E+9,9E+9,9E
-188.539,-151.177,616.111],[0,0,1,0],[-1,-1,0,0],[9E+9,9E+9,9E+9,9E+9,9E+9,9E
-190.91,-146.988,615.88],[0,0,1,0],[-1,-1,0,0],[9E+9,9E+9,9E+9,9E+9,9E+9,9E+9
-192.629,-143.95,615.686],[0,0,1,0],[-1,-1,0,0],[9E+9,9E+9,9E+9,9E+9,9E+9,9E+
-194.642,-140.394,615.535],[0,0,1,0],[-1,-1,0,0],[9E+9,9E+9,9E+9,9E+9,9E+9,9E
-196.654,-136.838,615.362],[0,0,1,0],[-1,-1,0,0],[9E+9,9E+9,9E+9,9E+9,9E+9,9E
-198.667,-133.282,615.155],[0,0,1,0],[-1,-1,0,0],[9E+9,9E+9,9E+9,9E+9,9E+9,9E
-200.679,-129.726,614.957],[0,0,1,0],[-1,-1,0,0],[9E+9,9E+9,9E+9,9E+9,9E+9,9E
-202.692,-126.17,614.726],[0,0,1,0],[-1,-1,0,0],[9E+9,9E+9,9E+9,9E+9,9E+9,9E+
-204.705,-122.614,614.353],[0,0,1,0],[-1,-1,0,0],[9E+9,9E+9,9E+9,9E+9,9E+9,9E
-206.319,-119.8,614.205],[0,0,1,0],[-1,-1,0,0],[9E+9,9E+9,9E+9,9E+9,9E+9,9E+9
-208.403,-116.687,613.767],[0,0,1,0],[-1,-1,0,0],[9E+9,9E+9,9E+9,9E+9,9E+9,9E
-212.246,-110.949,612.93],[0,0,1,0],[-1,-1,0,0],[9E+9,9E+9,9E+9,9E+9,9E+9,9E+
-214.753,-107.204,612.393],[0,0,1,0],[-1,-1,0,0],[9E+9,9E+9,9E+9,9E+9,9E+9,9E
-217.134,-103.648,612.187],[0,0,1,0],[-1,-1,0,0],[9E+9,9E+9,9E+9,9E+9,9E+9,9E
-219.358,-100.328,611.956],[0,0,1,0],[-1,-1,0,0],[9E+9,9E+9,9E+9,9E+9,9E+9,9E
-221.103,-97.722,612.064],[0,0,1,0],[-1,-1,0,0],[9E+9,9E+9,9E+9,9E+9,9E+9,9E+
-222.914,-95.094,612.481],[0,0,1,0],[-1,-1,0,0],[9E+9,9E+9,9E+9,9E+9,9E+9,9E+
-225.284,-92.358,612.372],[0,0,1,0],[-1,-1,0,0],[9E+9,9E+9,9E+9,9E+9,9E+9,9E+
-227.655,-89.691,612.545],[0,0,1,0],[-1,-1,0,0],[9E+9,9E+9,9E+9,9E+9,9E+9,9E+
-230.026,-87.614,612.667],[0,0,1,0],[-1,-1,0,0],[9E+9,9E+9,9E+9,9E+9,9E+9,9E+
-232.396,-85.537,612.849],[0,0,1,0],[-1,-1,0,0],[9E+9,9E+9,9E+9,9E+9,9E+9,9E+
-234.723,-83.498,613.78],[0,0,1,0],[-1,-1,0,0],[9E+9,9E+9,9E+9,9E+9,9E+9,9E+9
-237.138,-81.9,615.038],[0,0,1,0],[-1,-1,0,0],[9E+9,9E+9,9E+9,9E+9,9E+9,9E+9]
-239.508,-80.332,617.144],[0,0,1,0],[-1,-1,0,0],[9E+9,9E+9,9E+9,9E+9,9E+9,9E+

5.

6.

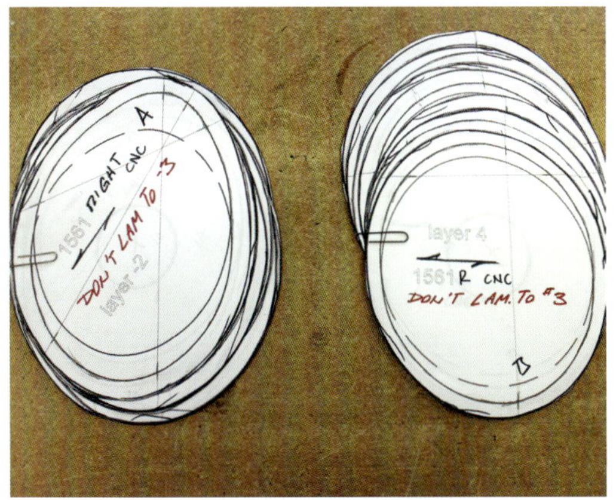
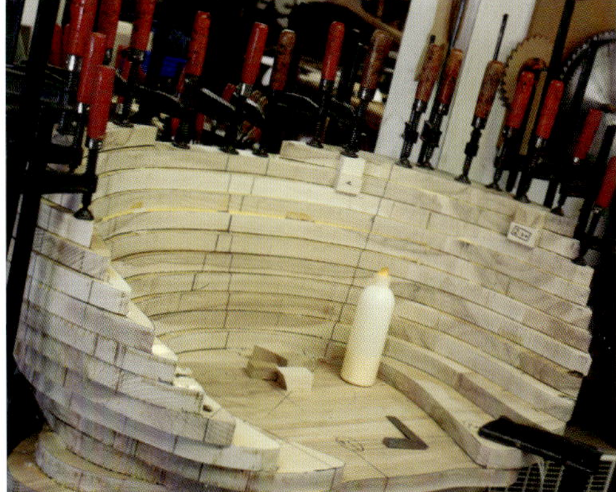

7.

10.

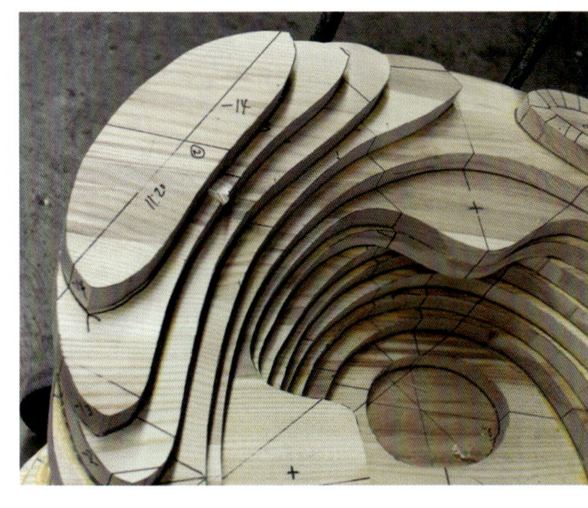

8.

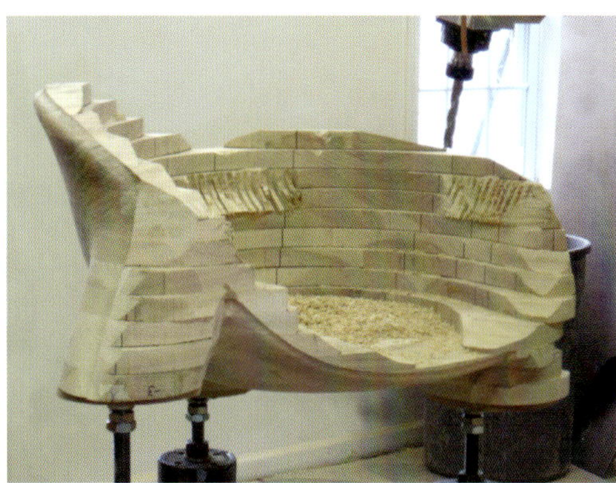
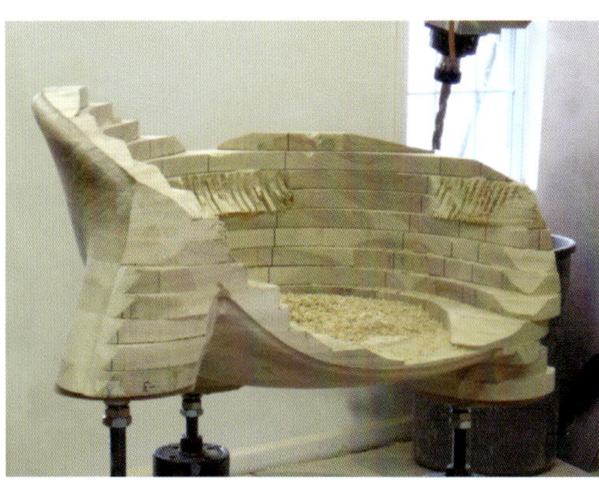

11.

9.

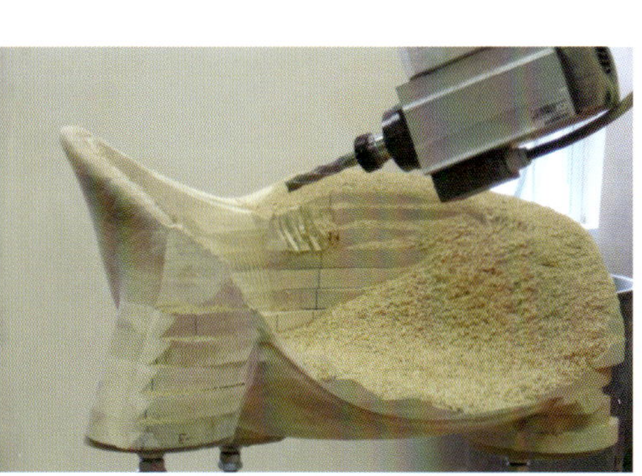
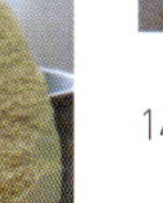

13.

14.

7. This group of cross sections indicates each of the successive laminate layers in one leg of *Long Night*.

8. After the cross sections are traced onto each slab of wood, they are cut out on the band saw. Here, the layers have been stacked and glued together, and are awaiting milling.

9. The stacked and glued laminate layers of *Long Night*'s body show guidelines that indicate the alignment of the layers, one to the next.

10. Based on the cross sections, the laminate layers of *Long Night*'s body have been cut out and glued together. Here, the addition of multiple clamps assists in making sure the layers adhere completely.

11. This is the CNC machine fit with a router, with the body of *Long Night* prepared for milling.

12. The CNC machine mills the rough laminate layers into the form of *Long Night*; now they are ready for hand detailing and finishing.

13. Although the CNC machine can achieve a level of precision, each piece will be hand detailed and finished.

14. Here, *Long Night* is completely milled and hand finished, waiting to be stained.

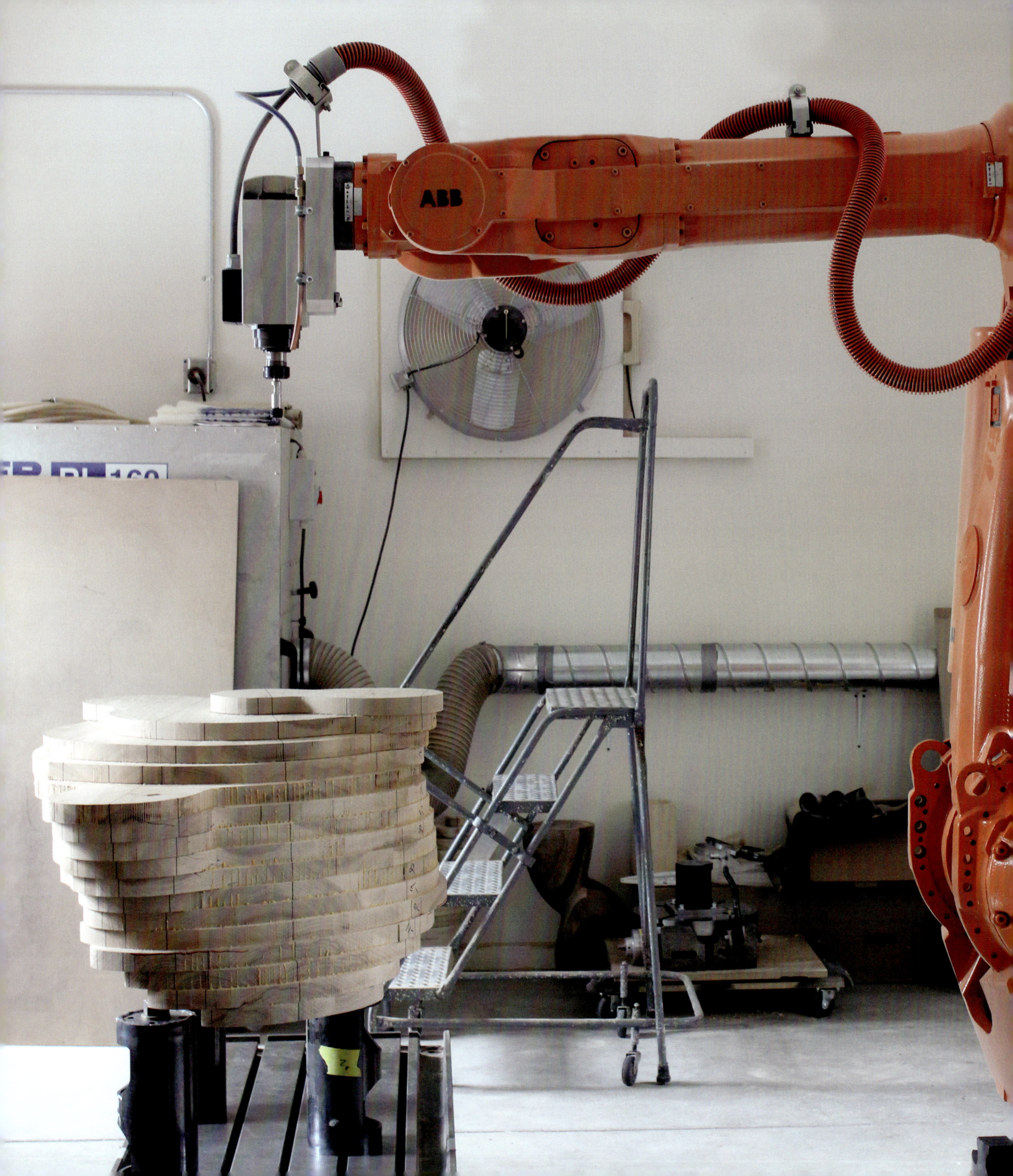

new design possibilities, Castle decided early on that the machine was not meant to drive his creative process but to partner with it. Similar to other tools used in the studio's practice, it was meant to fade into the background, invisible to the final form. "How the technology comes into this is something I'm very interested in . . . but I don't think of this as a 'crafting' technology. I think the end product is more important and if any of these things stand out—like the technology—then it's too much. You may not even think we are using any technology, even though we are. It won't be obvious, the work that the Robot does . . . in the end no one will know that the Robot will do anything," says Castle.[8]

For those interested in how computational tools intertwine with the traditional practices of creative work, the Castle studio paints an enlivened picture of tools being worked against their grain, meeting the practitioner in a space that sparks and evolves creative endeavor. While Castle's new pieces are not driven by the recent technological prowess of the studio, they are more grand, complex, and imaginative than ever, in part because of the new possibilities and "conversations" these tools afford. Thus, as digital-fabrication tools have shifted some of the work into largely unfamiliar algorithmic spaces and work flows, they have also moved forward a much older program of work, expanding and renewing the Castle studio's long effort to liberate the wood from its inherent physical properties.

Castle, who launched his career during an era that tended to celebrate the "creative genius" laboring alone in the studio with his carving tools and materials, offers us a new way of looking at creative practice within the art-furniture movement. His expanded creative workflow now includes processes and methods more aligned with contemporary digital-art practices (or indeed, industrial manufacturing), while still honoring the properties of organic forms, materials, and human craft. In some ways, this represents a break with the past, but in others it promotes a further cementing of Castle's considerable reputation as both craftsman and innovator. That his emerging practice can support both evaluations simultaneously speaks to the complexity of craft transitions in a post-digital era.

1. Tim Ingold, "The Textility of Making," *Cambridge Journal of Economics* 34, no. 1 (May 2009): 92–97.

2. Steven J. Jackson and Laewoo Kang, "Breakdown, Obsolescence and Reuse: HCI and the Art of Repair," (paper presented at the SIGCHI Conference on Human Factors in Computing Systems, Toronto, Canada, April 1, 2014).

3. Amy Cheatle and Steven J. Jackson, "Digital Entanglements: Craft, Computation and Collaboration in Fine Arts Furniture Production" (paper presented at the 2015 Computer Supported Cooperative Work (CSCW) Conference, Vancouver, BC, February 2015).

4. Author's interview with Wendell Castle, Rochester, NY, March 22, 2014.

5. Author's interview with Wendell Castle, Rochester, NY, May 20, 2014.

6. Author's interview with Castle, Rochester, NY, March 22, 2014.

7. Author's interview with Marvin Pallischeck, Rochester, NY, May 20, 2014.

8. Author's interview with Castle, May 20, 2014.

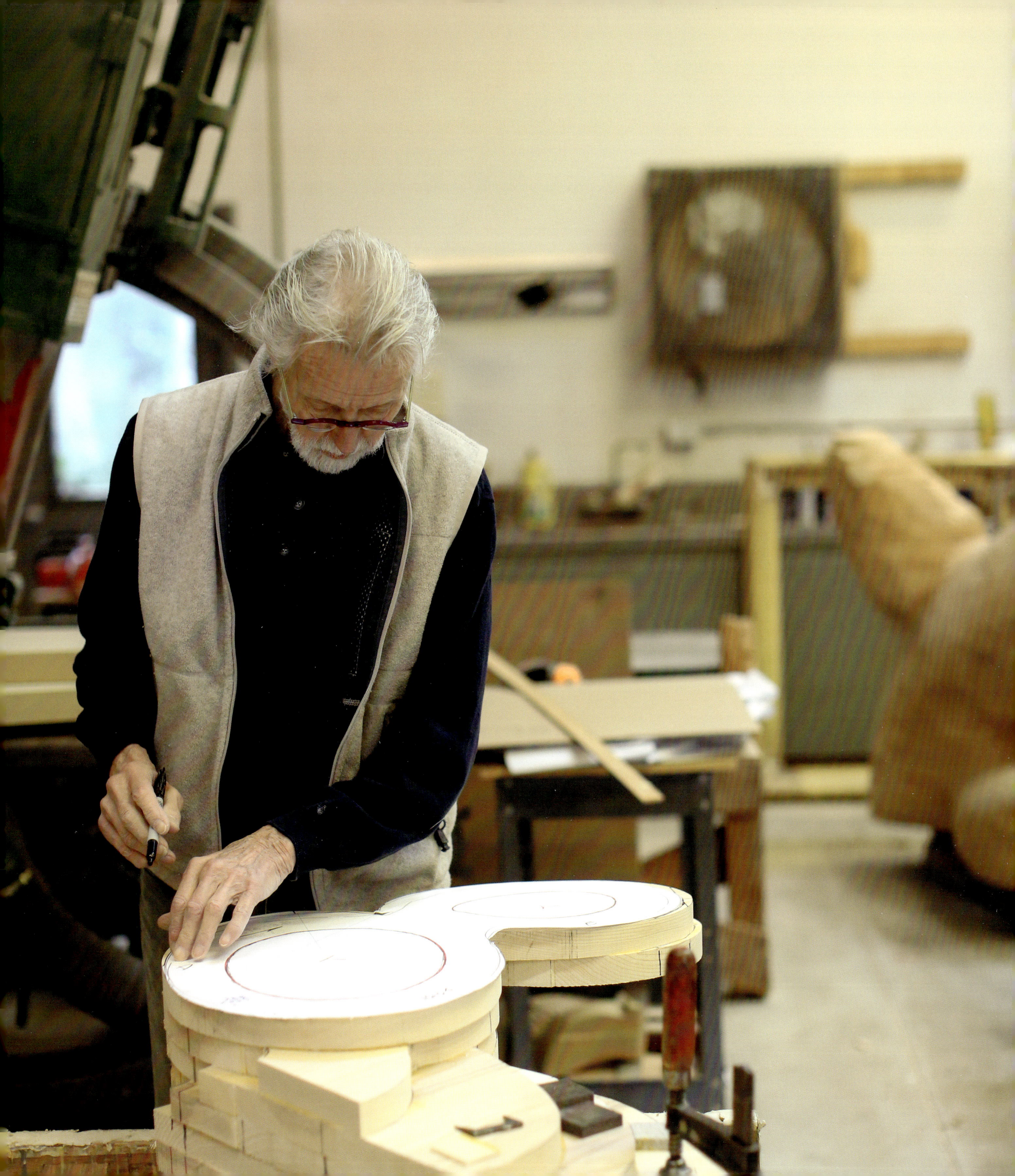

Process

THIS SECTION ILLUSTRATES the various stages that each piece must go through, from initial sketch to the final surface treatment. At any given moment, Wendell Castle and his assistants work on several different pieces simultaneously. It may take weeks or up to nine months to complete a piece depending on the complexity of the work. The Robot is not always used. The images were photographed over seven various studio visits in 2014 and 2015, capturing multiple works in different stages of production.

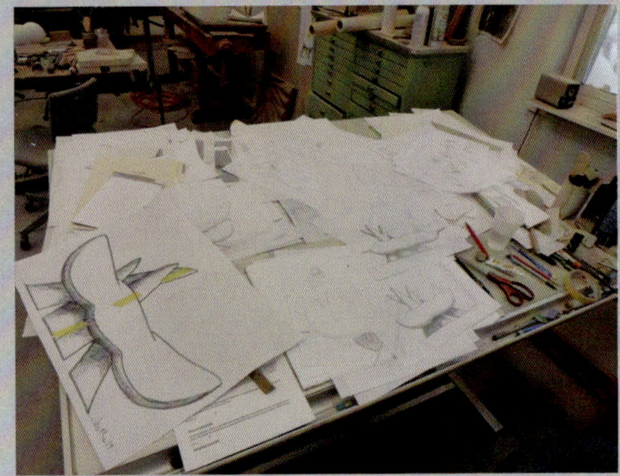

1. Castle's drawing table in his studio with various sketches in process.

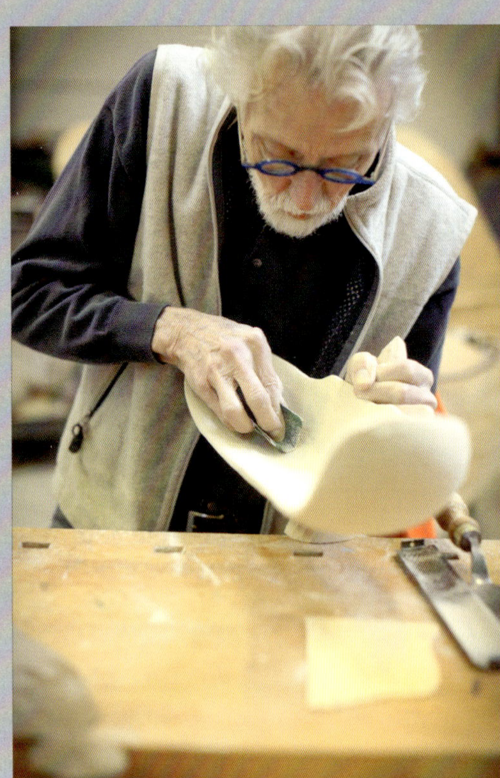

2. Castle sanding the seat of a urethane signfoam model of *Grand Temptation* (2014).

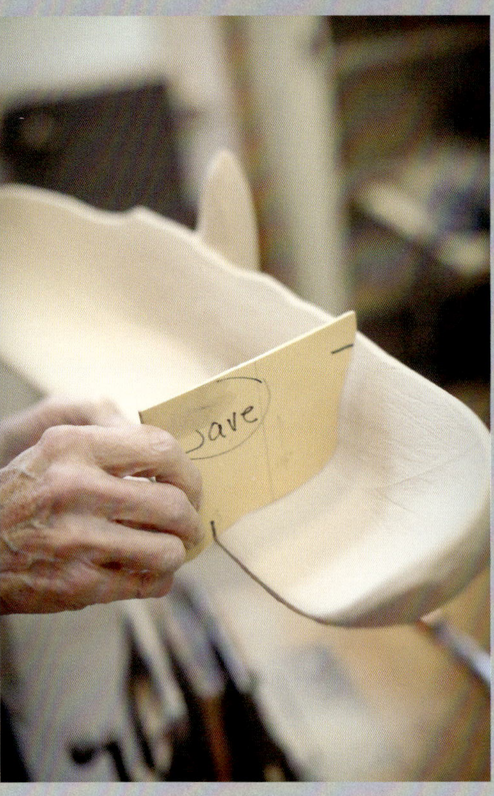

3. Castle measuring the seat depth on the urethane signfoam model of *Grand Temptation* (2014).

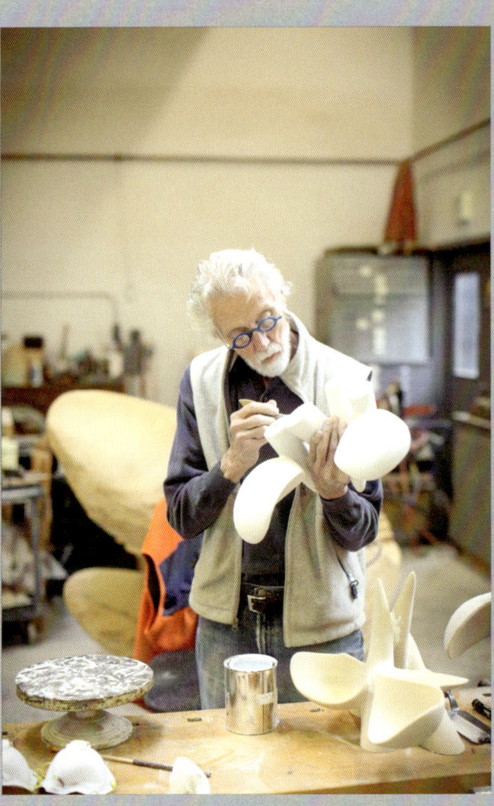

4. Castle painting the urethane signfoam model of *No Bounds* (n.d.) in preparation for 3D scanning.

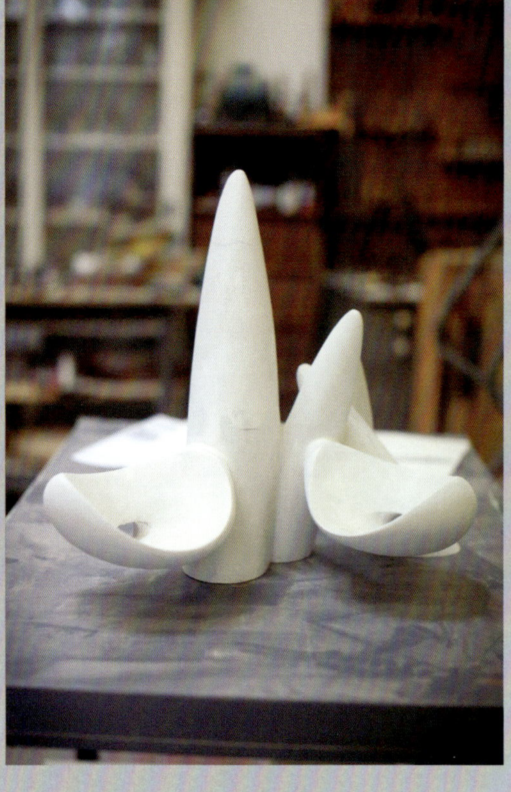

5. Urethane signfoam model of *Wandering Mountain* (2014, plate 27).

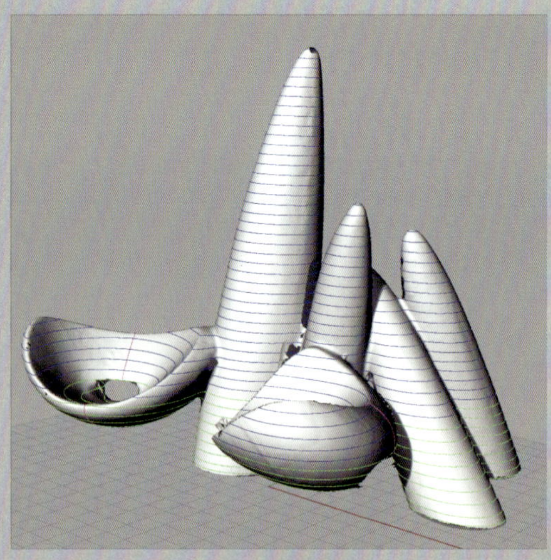

6. Computer-aided-design (CAD) digital model of *Wandering Mountain* (2014) showing laminate layers.

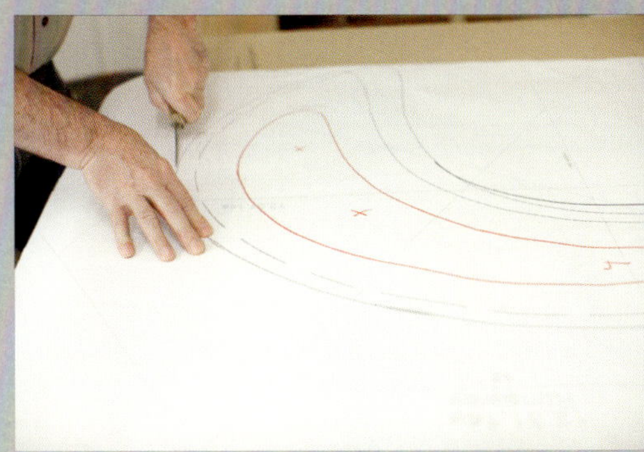

7. A cross section, freshly printed off the architectural plotter, is cut out.

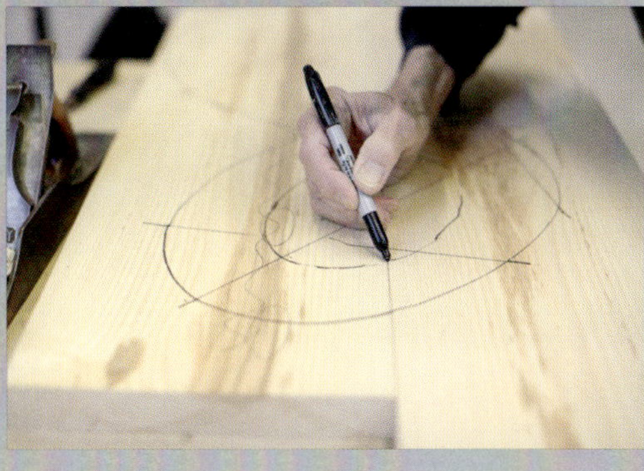

10. Castle highlighting a pattern on a wooden board for cutting on the band saw.

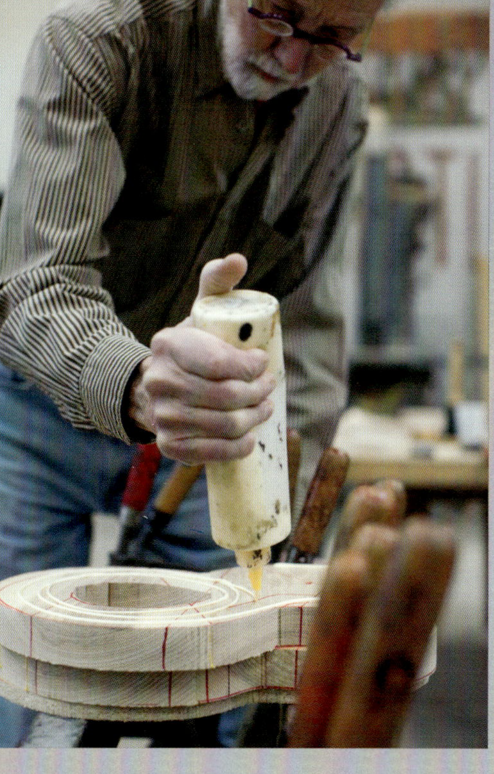

13. Castle "gluing up" or adhering layers of lamination together.

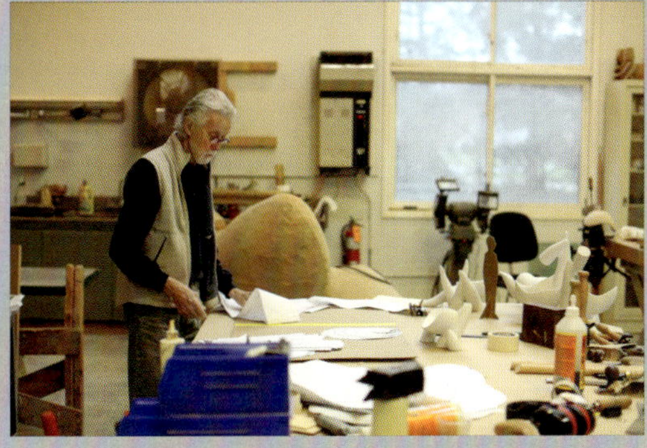

8. Castle organizing paper templates for lamination.

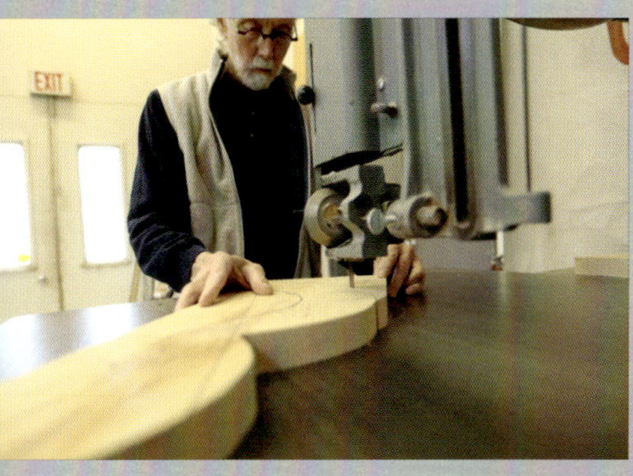

11. Castle cutting out a laminate layer in ash on the band saw.

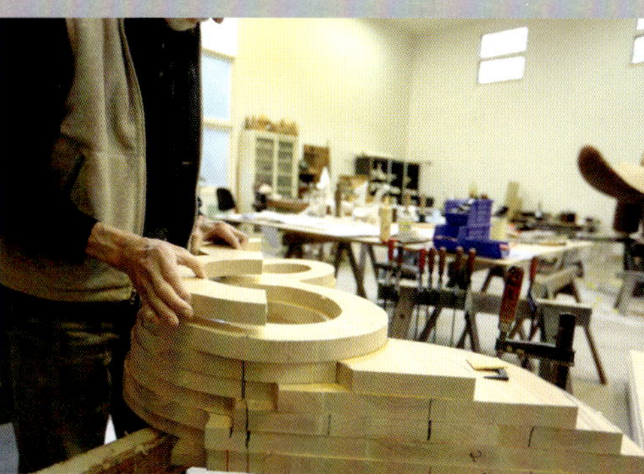

14. Castle fitting layers of lamination together.

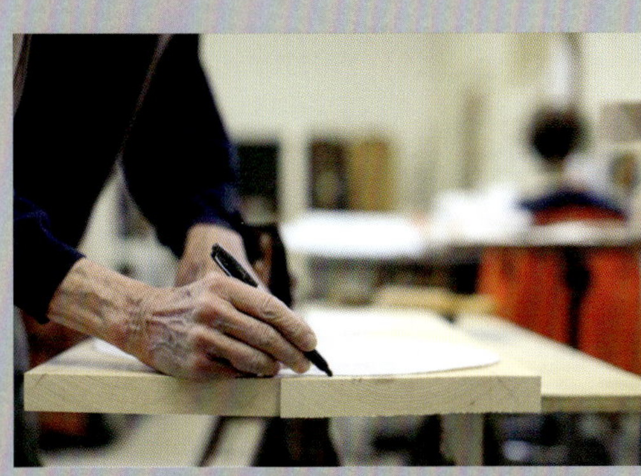

9. Castle tracing a lamination template onto a wooden board for cutting.

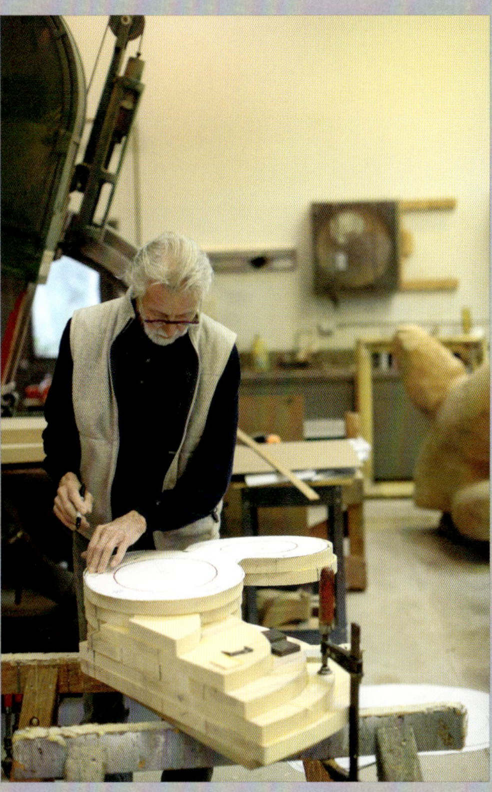

12. Castle verifying the orientation of the laminations.

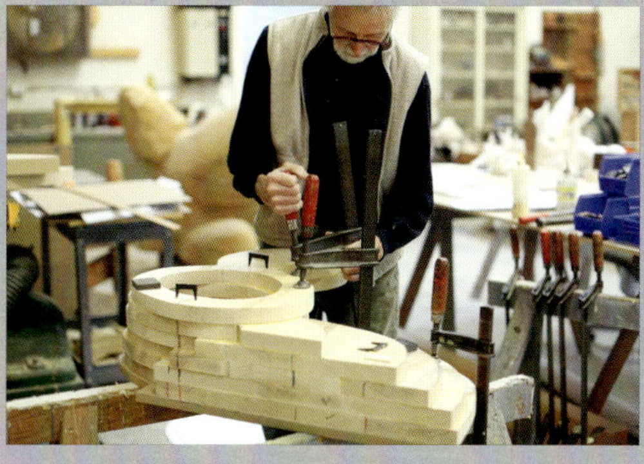

15. Castle clamping glued lamination layers together so that they adhere fully.

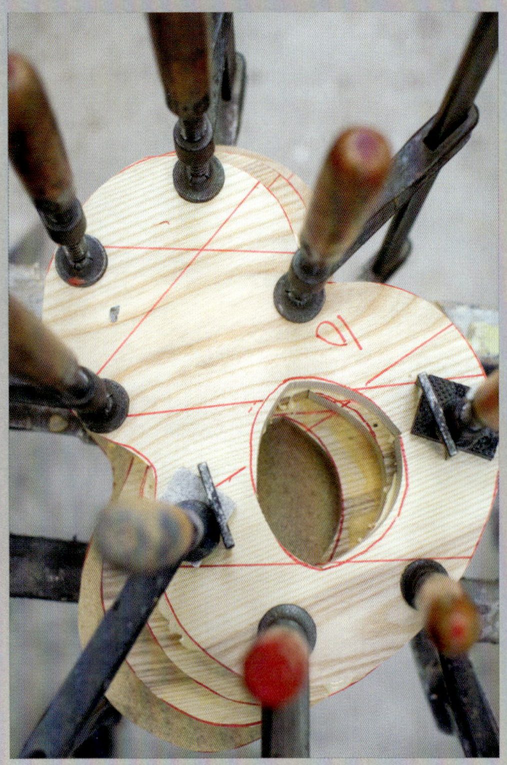

16. Clamped laminated ash waiting for the glue to dry.

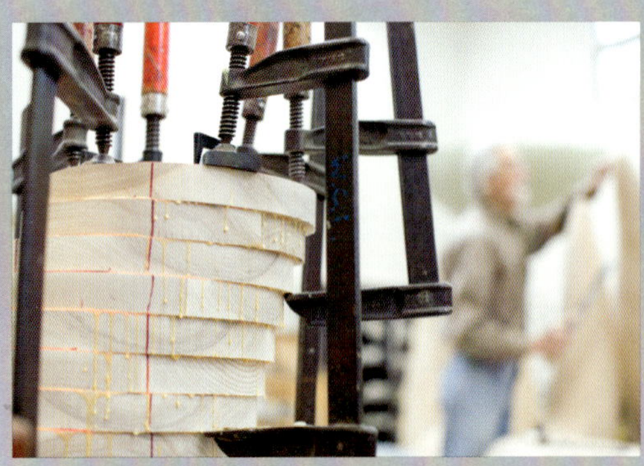

17. Side view of stack-laminated work with glue drying.

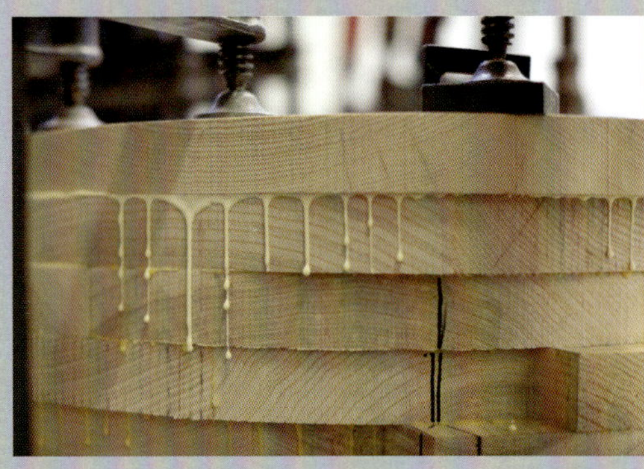

18. Close-up of clamped and glued lamination layers.

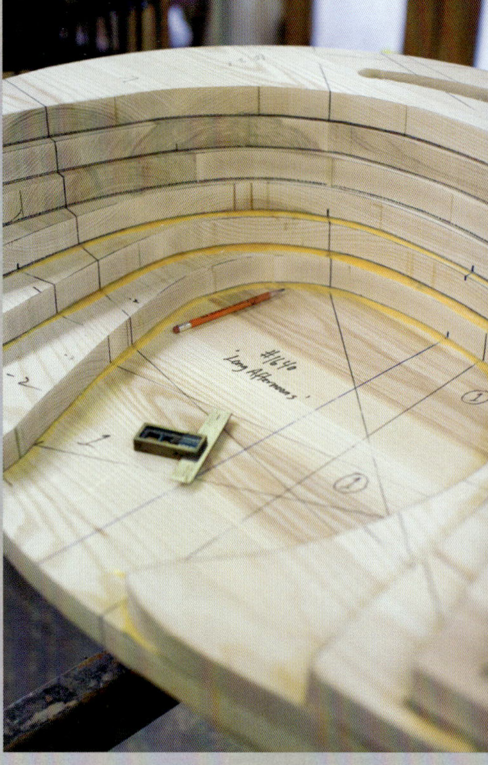

19. Close-up of the seat for *Long Afternoon* (2015), partially laminated and illustrating the alignment of the layers.

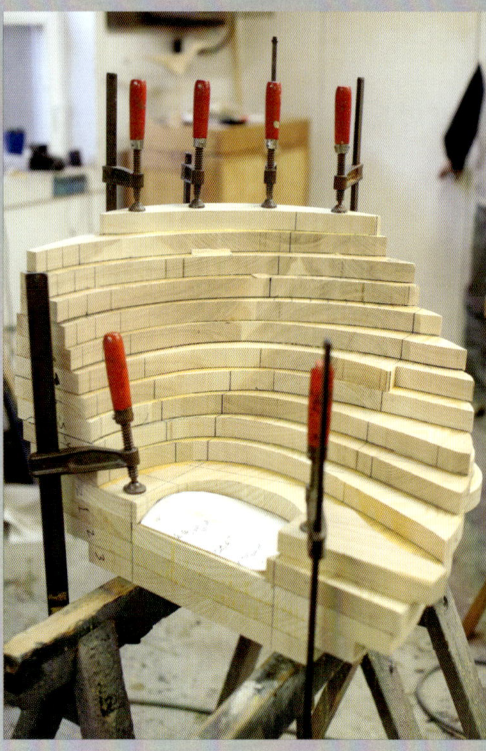

20. Laminated seat of half of *Crossroads* (2014) glued and clamped for drying.

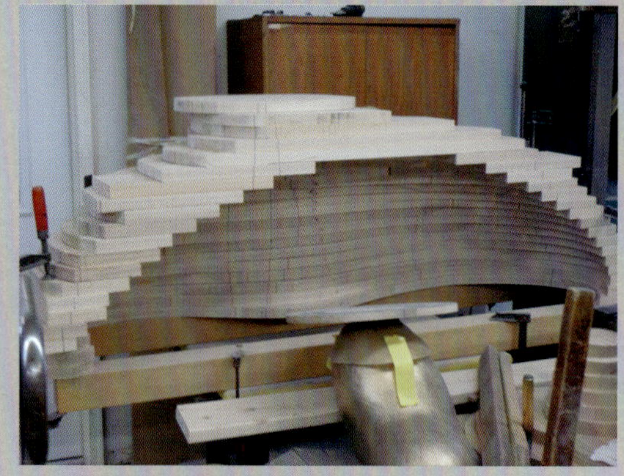

21. Laminate layers awaiting milling.

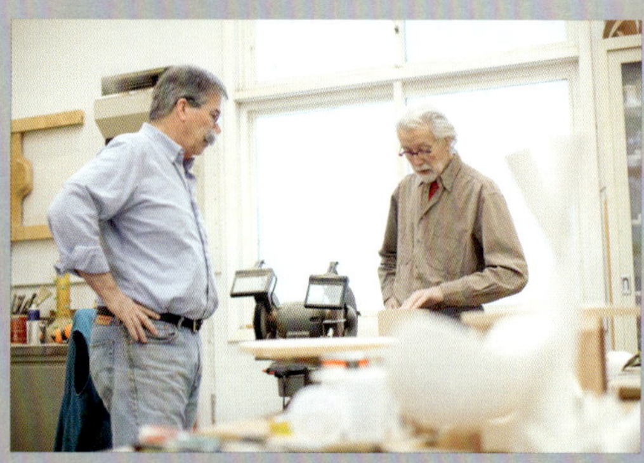

22. Castle and Marvin Pallischeck, Castle's studio manager, discussing model work.

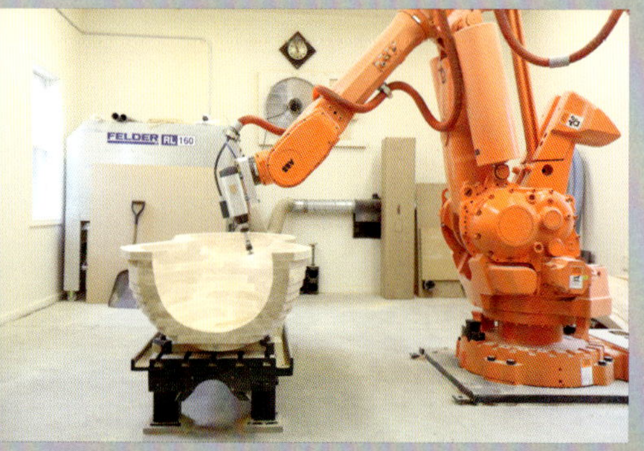

23. The computer-numerical-control (CNC) machine, dubbed Mr. Chips, milling out the interior of the cabinet component of *Remembering You* (2015, plate 6).

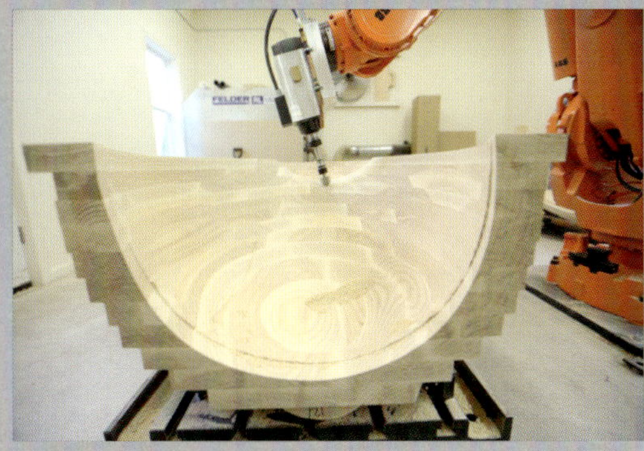

24. Close-up of the CNC machine, dubbed Mr. Chips, milling out the interior of the cabinet component of *Remembering You* (2015).

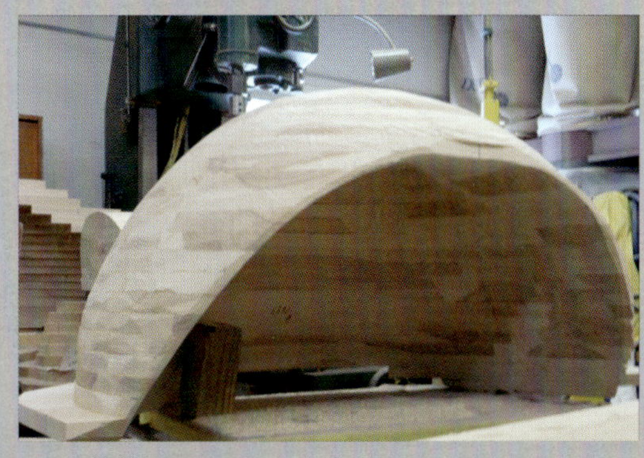

25. The seat for *Tempted* (2015) after milling has been completed by the CNC machine, Mr. Chips, and awaiting handwork.

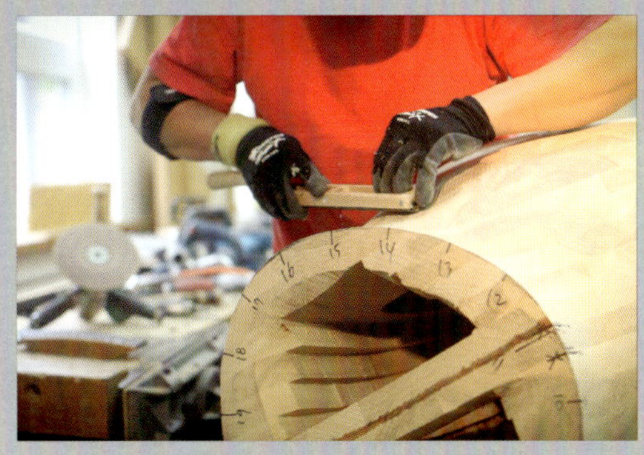

26. Studio assistant "sure-forming" or making sure the form and finishing of *High Hopes* (2015, plate 12) is precise and accurate.

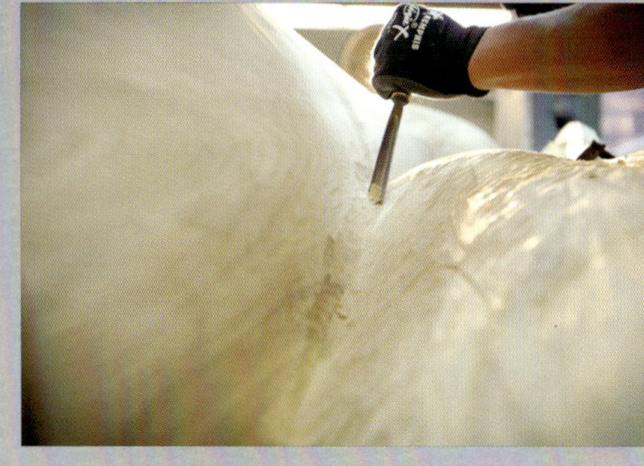

27. Studio assistant chip-carving the body of *I'll Fly Away* (2013) after it has been milled.

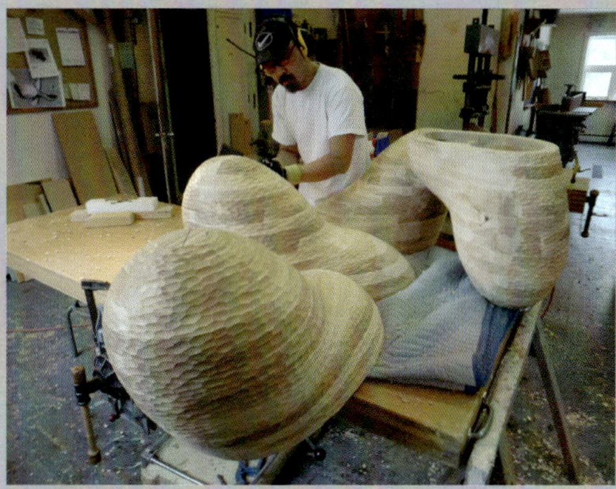

28. Tae-Youl Ryu chip-carving the leg of *Starstruck* (2014), a coffee table made in ash.

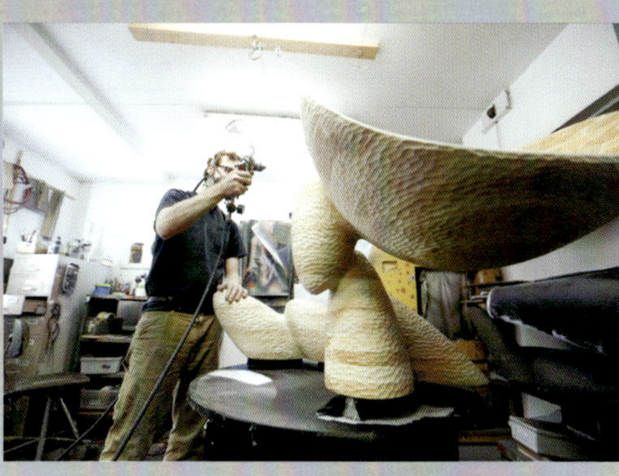

29. Matthew Klock, a studio assistant who works in finishing, pre-wetting a work with water to prepare it for staining.

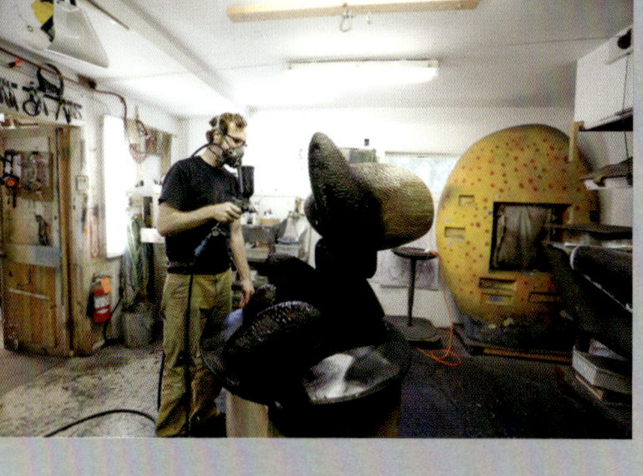

30. Klock is applying a water-based indicator stain.

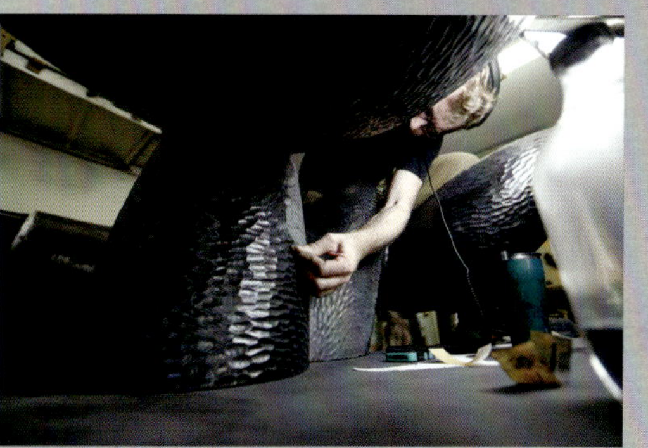

31. Klock is smoothing out aberrant textures from carve marks and adding a sanding tooth prior to applying a coat of oil-fill.

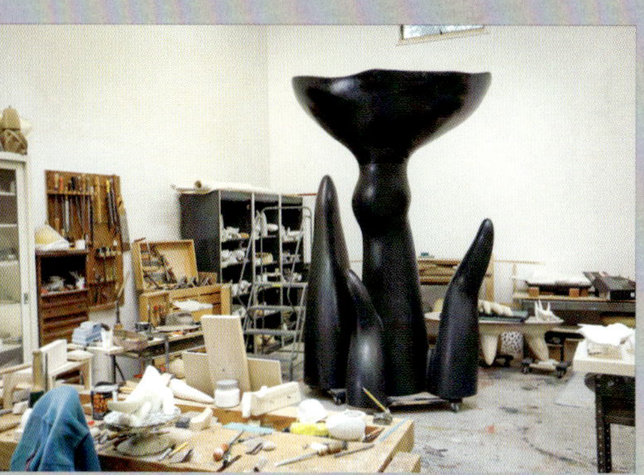

32. A finished work, *High Hopes* (2015), in Castle's studio.

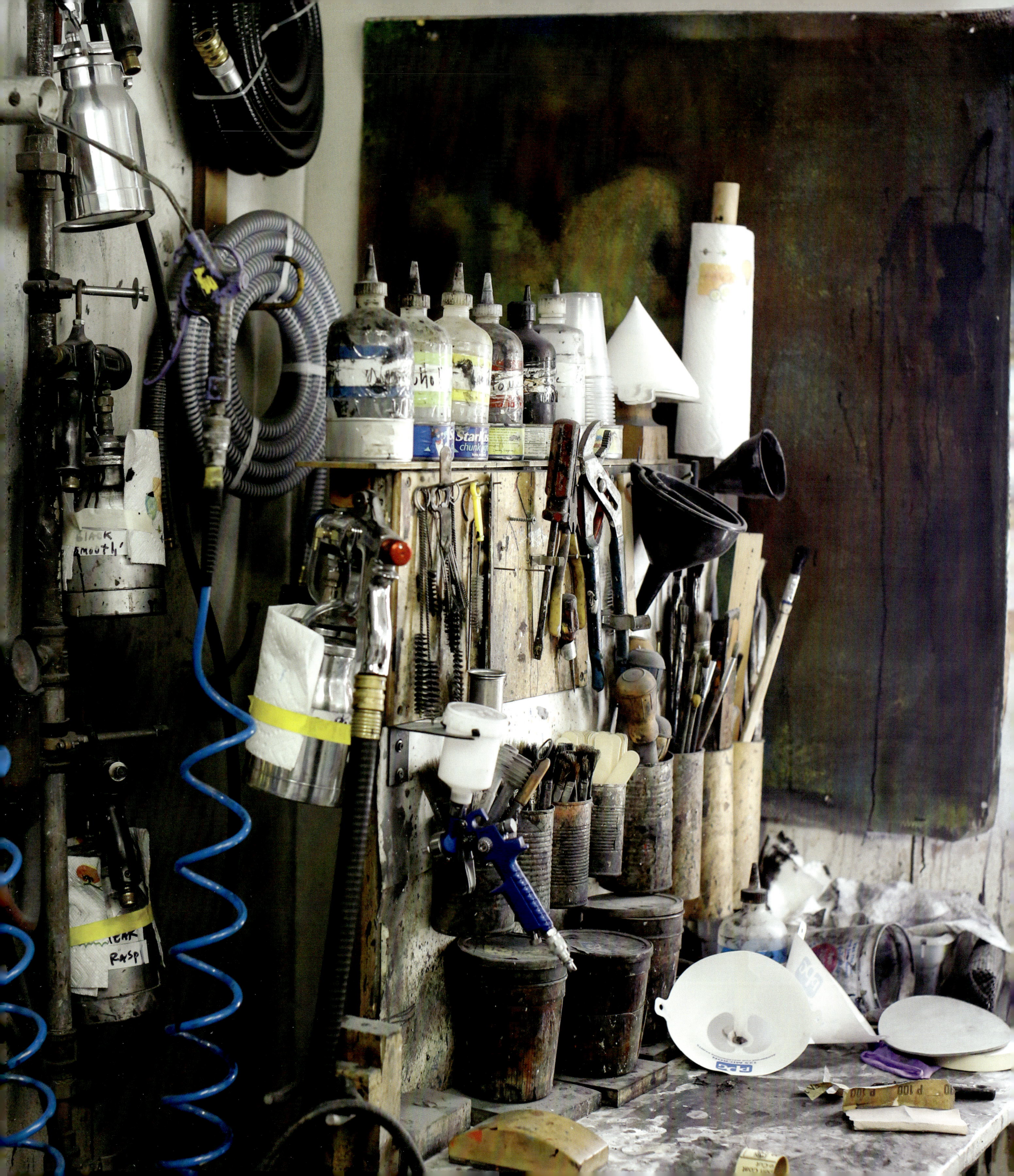

BLACK
SMOOTH'
CLEAR
RASP